The Mystery of Criminal Behavior—Obstacles to Solving the Enigma

The Mystery of Criminal Behavior—Obstacles to Solving the Enigma

Thomas G. Toombs, PhD

iUniverse, Inc.

New York Lincoln Shanghai

The Mystery of Criminal Behavior—Obstacles to Solving the Enigma

Copyright © 2007 by Thomas G. Toombs

iUniverse books may be ordered through booksellers or by contacting:

iUniverse
2021 Pine Lake Road, Suite 100
Lincoln, NE 68512
www.iuniverse.com
1-800-Authors (1-800-288-4677)

ISBN-13: 978-0-595-41592-2 (pbk)
ISBN-13: 978-0-595-85940-5 (ebk)
ISBN-10: 0-595-41592-X (pbk)
ISBN-10: 0-595-85940-2 (ebk)

Printed in the United States of America

To Dexter

A farmer at heart, he had the soul of a poet.
May 24, 1941–March 10, 2005

Contents

Tables

Preface

In San Jose, California, there is a place called the Winchester Mystery House. The house was built and occupied by Sarah L. Winchester, the widow of William Wirt Winchester, whose family company invented the Winchester rifle. In grief over the premature deaths of her infant daughter and husband, Mrs. Winchester consulted a spiritualist. Legend has it that the spiritualist contacted Mr. Winchester in the afterworld. The late Mr. Winchester supposedly told the spiritualist to tell his wife that his death and the death of their daughter had been caused by the spirits of those who had been killed by the Winchester rifle, and that she too was in danger of meeting the same fate. Mr. Winchester instructed his wife through the spiritualist that to avoid the curse which had befallen him and their daughter, she must build a home in which both she and the restless spirits would live, or she too would die. For thirty-six years, until just after Mrs. Winchester died in her sleep, twenty-two carpenters worked around the clock on every day of the year—building, demolishing, and remodeling the house (Taylor 2001).

The result is a structural monstrosity, filled with architectural oddities that have neither logic nor purpose. The house is seven stories tall, contains 160 rooms, forty-seven fireplaces, doorways that open into blank walls, stairways leading nowhere, chimneys that do not penetrate the ceiling, trap doors to nowhere, hallways that double back on themselves, skylights mounted one on top of another, exterior doors with no porch or steps, stair posts installed upside down, and a forty-two-step winding stairway—which normally would rise three stories—that rises only nine feet because each riser is only two inches high.

In many respects, the process used to construct America's corrections system has been analogous to the process used by Mrs. Winchester to construct her house; and so too are the corresponding results. Like the construction process that built the Winchester Mystery House, the construction process that has built America's corrections system has been driven by advice—advice provided not by spiritualists, but by a variety of sources, some of which are not much more reliable than spiritualists. Archival records, library shelves, legislative hearing records, and the Internet are filled with books, journal articles, and other written accounts that contain theories and ideas regarding the causes of criminal behavior and what can be done to prevent it that have been advanced over time by a multitude of philosophers, scholars, intellectuals, students, practitioners, judges, prosecuting attorneys, defense lawyers, journalists, ex-offenders, victims, police officers, private citizen advisory groups, individual concerned citizens, and political leaders.

Based originally on the principle of punishment, the corrections system has been periodically remodeled to incorporate the principles of penitence, reform, rehabilitation, resocialization, reintegration, and restoration. Each renovation has been made without regard for form or function. The end result is a system supported by a hodgepodge of governing principles and philosophies, none of which can explain what causes criminal behavior or how to prevent it.

The bizarre nature of America's corrections system appears even more bizarre and unmanageable when contrasted with corrections systems in most other Western countries. Whereas the corrections systems of most of the Western world answer to a single government authority, the American corrections system is fragmented. In the United States, the federal government, individual state governments, and many local governments operate jails, prisons, and other corrections programs that are totally independent of one another. There are no uniform policies or standards that govern correctional practices at all levels of government in the United States.

In 1974, the American Correctional Association—a multi-disciplinary organization comprised of professionals representing every component of the criminal justice system, academia, and the citizenry at large—promulgated a series of standards for correctional agencies (federal, state, and local) that administer corrections programs or operate correctional facilities. These standards address services, programs, and operations that are considered essential to good correctional management—administrative and fiscal controls, staff training and development, physical-plant management, safety and emergency procedures, sanitation, food service, and rules of conduct and discipline. The purpose of these standards is to promote uniformity and consistency in the policies, procedures, and practices of correctional agencies nationwide. These standards are reviewed twice a year by an accreditation commission, and are amended when necessary. The adoption of and compliance with these standards is, however, voluntary. The policies and practices used to govern the operation of most correctional programs and facilities are left to the discretion of elected and appointed government officials at the federal, state, and local levels.

America's corrections system, like the Winchester Mystery House is certainly an interesting one. It contains remnants of every era of criminal-justice thinking. Unlike the Winchester Mystery House, however, America's corrections system remains under construction; and there is still no consensus as to what purpose it should serve, what the final structure should look like, or how it should be operated.

Introduction

Criminal behavior has an enormous socioeconomic impact on society. According to the 2005 edition of *Crime in the United States*—published annually by the United States Department of Justice—there were a total of 11,695,264 crimes committed in the United States in 2004: 1,367,009 violent crimes and 10,328,255 property crimes. The Department of Justice defines violent crime as one of four offenses: murder and non-negligent manslaughter, forcible rape, robbery, and aggravated assault. Property crimes include burglary, larceny, motor-vehicle theft. The data indicates that in 2004, a violent crime was committed somewhere in the country every 23.1 seconds; and a property crime was committed every 3.1 seconds. The majority of crimes—more than 85 percent—were property crimes. These estimates are based on the number of arrests made, not on the number of convictions.

Crime rates in the United States vary somewhat between geographic regions. The Justice Department has divided the country into four regions: the Northeast, Midwest, Southern, and Western regions. The following tables list the estimated rates of crime, by type, experienced by each region of the country during 2004.

Table 1: Northeast Region

Estimated Property Crime: 2358.9 per 100,000 inhabitants

Estimated Violent Crime: 390.7 per 100,000 inhabitants

Table 2: Midwest Region

Estimated Property Crime: 3281 per 100,000 inhabitants

Estimated Violent Crime: 391.1 per 100,000 inhabitants

Table 3: Southern Region

Estimated Property Crime: 4002.2 per 100,000 inhabitants

Estimated Violent Crime: 540.6 per 100,000 inhabitants

Table 4: Western Region

Estimated Property Crime: 3891.2 per 100,000 inhabitants

Estimated Violent Crime: 480.7 per 100,000 inhabitants

The distribution of crime by age, gender, and race is also based on arrest data, not convictions. In 2005, the United States Department of Justice reported that 53.2 percent of the people arrested in 2004 were between the ages of fifteen and twenty-nine. The largest single group of those arrested (15.8 percent of the total) was eighteen or younger. The next largest group of those arrested (13 percent) were people between the ages of twenty-five and twenty-nine. People between the ages of thirty and forty-four accounted for less than one-third (29.5 percent) of all arrests. Only 12.3 percent of people arrested were 45 or older. In terms of gender, 75.8 percent of those arrested in 2004 were male, and 24.2 percent were female. Arrest distribution by race reveals that 68.5 percent of all arrestees were white, 29.1 percent were black, and 2.4 percent were of other races (Asian, Pacific Islander, Native American, or Alaskan Native).

For record-keeping purposes, the federal government refers to crimes solved as "crimes cleared." Crimes can be cleared in one of two ways. First, a crime may be cleared when at least one person is arrested, charged, and remanded to the court for prosecution. Second, a crime may be cleared by what the government calls "exceptional means," which applies "when some force outside the agency's control prevents the arrest of the individual." No conviction is required in order to clear a crime.

In 2004, less than half (43.7 percent) of the estimated 1,367,009 violent crimes committed in the United States were solved or cleared, and nearly half of the cleared crimes (46.3 percent) were cleared by exceptional means. The estimated percentage of 2004 property crimes reported cleared was even lower than that of violent crimes. Nationwide, just 16.5 percent of the estimated 10,328,255 property crimes committed in 2004 were reported cleared by arrest or exceptional means.

At the end of 2004, the estimated total number of adult criminals in the United States who were under supervision by a federal, state, or local government correctional agency was 7,102,710. Criminals incarcerated in either a state or federal prison totaled 1,438,701. Another 747,529 were confined in local jails; 4,151,125 were on probation; and 765,355 were on parole. An estimated 3.2 percent of the resident population of the United States over the age of eighteen—or approximately one in every thirty-two people in a population of 220,377.406—were either incarcerated or under the supervision of probation[1] or parole authorities in January 2005. It is evident from these data that demographically, all of American society—except perhaps the very young and the very old—engages to some degree in criminal activity.

---

1   The terms probationer and parolee are often mistakenly used as though they are synonymous. Probationers are criminal offenders who have been sentenced to a period of conditional supervision in the community. Parolees are criminal offenders who have been released to a period of conditional supervision after serving a period of time in prison.

In addition to the negative social consequences of crime, there is a great financial burden on taxpayers, who must pay the cost of operating the existing criminal justice system. This cost, plus the dollar losses caused by physical injuries, emotional trauma, loss of life, and damage to property experienced by victims of crime, amounts to an astronomical sum. The estimated cost of crime varies, depending on the formula used to calculate it. The formula used by the United States Department of Justice takes into account victims' losses as a result of property theft or damage, cash losses, medical expenses, and income loss due to injuries received from the crime; as well as total government expenditures—federal, state, and local—for police protection, corrections, judicial services, and legal activities. Using this formula, the Department of Justice has estimated that the cost of crime in 2003 was more than $200 billion—$20 billion in victims' losses and $185 billion in government expenditures. Economist David Anderson has estimated that the aggregate cost of crime— which, he says, is not limited to the operating cost of the criminal justice system and victims' losses, but also includes the opportunity costs of time lost by victims, criminals, and prisoners; the cost of private deterrence; and losses caused by citizens' fear of being victimized—is more than $1.7 trillion per annum. No matter which estimate is used, the outcome is the same: crime is costly (Hughes 2006; Hughes 1994; Anderson 2004).

I have spent 30 years as a corrections practitioner, operating institutions and administering programs for juvenile offenders, adult criminals, and the criminally insane. Throughout this time, there was an ever-present aura of tension and uncertainty surrounding my work that was a by-product of the ongoing disagreement between those who promote a "get tough" approach to crime, and those who take exception to this philosophy and argue for a less punitive approach. In correctional parlance, this dichotomy is referred to as "punishment versus treatment." Some characterize the struggle between punishment and treatment as being analogous to the motion of a pendulum swinging back and forth between two extremes. However, if the course of shifting correctional philosophy really were analogous to the course of a pendulum, it would be possible to monitor its path, determine its line, measure its speed, and predict when a change in direction will occur. This is not the case. The conflict between advocates for punishment and advocates for treatment is more analogous to a mobile that swirls, darts, bobs, and skips, unpredictably changing direction in response to the winds of change—winds driven by myths, intuition, and the prerogatives of power.

A number of books have been written that discuss and promote particular theoretical approaches to corrections. This book does not serve the same purpose. Instead, this book critically analyzes the theories most commonly promoted in the literature and practiced in the field, which generally represent one of two schools of thought: classical and positivist. It concludes that none of the theories advocated to date have produced or offer promising results, and asserts that there are at least three major obstacles—pseudoscientific research practices; prisons; and intellectual and ideological parochialism—that must be overcome before any progress can be made toward discovering the cause(s) of criminal behavior, and determining how to prevent it.

My hope is that this book will be educational to the misinformed and the uninformed, compromising to those who distort or misrepresent what is known about criminal behavior, and motivational to those who are sincere in their pursuit of a solution.

Part 1

The Classical School

Chapter 1

HISTORICAL FOUNDATION AND
THEORETICAL OVERVIEW

The cornerstone of the "classical school" of corrections
philosophy is the belief that criminal behavior is an expres-
sion of free will, a voluntary act committed after careful
consideration of the consequences. The most effective
remedy for crime according to classical school thinkers is
punishment. The concept of punishment and its capacity
to alter behavior have been the subject of speculation for
centuries by scholars and thinkers such as Cesare Beccaria,
Jeremy Bentham, Voltaire, Denis Diderot, David Hume,
Adam Smith, Thomas Paine, Immanuel Kant, Georg
Wilhelm Hegel, and Friedrich Nietzsche. (Bentham 1996;
Maestro 1972; Berlin 1956; Beardsley 1988; Skinner
1999; and Thorndike 2002).

Although there are subtle differences in their ideology,
most classical school scholars seem to agree that for punishment to be effective—that is to deter others from committing crimes and to prevent a criminal from becoming a
repeat offender—a relationship must be established
between the crime committed and the punishment

imposed. To achieve this end, three things must happen. First, punishment must be swift. The more time that elapses between the commission of a crime and the imposition of punishment, the less likely it becomes that the punishment will alter an offender's behavior or deter others from engaging in criminal behavior. Second, punishment must be certain. For criminal behavior to be effectively deterred, an individual must believe that the probability of being caught is too high, and the degree of punishment too painful to take the risk. Third, punishment should not be applied in retaliation or out of vengeance. Rather, punishment should be applied to prevent the criminal from committing other crimes, and by example deter others from committing crimes. The method of punishment should be that which serves the greatest public good. The more serious the crime, classical school thinkers argue, the more severe the punishment should be.

The philosophy of the classical school has never been totally displaced by other approaches. One of the more popular theories advanced in recent times is Rational Choice Theory, also known as Situational Theory or Control Theory 2. According to this theory, all people are selfishly motivated. Each person identifies his or her own wants and desires, prioritizes them, and selects a means of achieving them that offer the greatest probability of success. Poverty, unemployment, broken homes, illiteracy, poor health care, or an injured psyche do not breed criminals, the theory postulates. These factors are merely excuses used by criminals to justify their behavior (Clarke & Mayhew 1980; Elster 1986; Jeffery 1971; and Scott 1999).

Proponents of the Rational Choice theory argue that if the commission of a crime is made difficult and the penalty for committing it is harsh, then anyone considering a criminal act will rationally decide it is not worth the effort required to commit the crime or to pay the consequence if caught. Strategies for effective crime prevention programs based on this theory require three fundamental elements: 1) discarding the idea that criminal behavior is caused by social, psychological, economic, or biological factors; 2) making it harder for crimes to be committed and easier for criminals to be caught; and 3) ensuring harsh punishment. Mandatory prison terms, the elimination of parole, life sentences after third felony convictions (so-called "three strikes" rule), and capital punishment are all strongly supported by proponents of this theory.

In order to make it harder for criminals to commit crimes, Rational Choice enthusiasts advocate mapping criminal activity and flooding the areas where most crime is committed with additional police, video surveillance systems, intrusion detection systems, and security patrols. Citizens are encouraged to install security hardware on the doors and windows of their homes and businesses, as well as to avail themselves of self-defense and firearms training.

Gloria Laycock, director of the Jill Dando Institute of Crime Science, a relatively new think tank established in 2001 at the University College of London (England), is certain that opportunity is the most significant and universal cause of crime, not poor parenting or inadequate education. Laycock argues—while acknowledging that it may be an over-generalization—that there are two kinds of criminals: the opportunistic criminal and the proper criminal. Opportunistic criminals are those criminals who act impulsively, without forethought or planning. Proper criminals are those criminals for whom crime is a business, which is carefully planned. Laycock says that most crimes are committed by opportunistic criminals, which can be prevented by altering and redesigning physical environments to make it harder to commit a crime, thereby increasing the risk of being caught and reducing the potential for reward (Laycock 2001).

Evidence of this approach to crime prevention can be seen in the increasing number of gated residential communities that have been constructed in the United States during the past twenty years. It could be argued that, universally applied, this approach to crime prevention would result in a kind of role reversal: non-criminals would be securely confined in walled, gated, and guarded compounds, while criminals would be free to roam the outer streets at will.

Chapter 2

METHODS OF PUNISHMENT

Probation

Probation is a form of sentencing that allows the criminal to live in the community, subject to conditions imposed by the court that are enforced by a supervising probation officer. In some instances, the criminal is required to complete a jail sentence (typically no more than one year) before being released on probation. Failure to satisfactorily complete the conditions of probation may result in the criminal being sentenced to a term in prison.

Although many people may not consider probation to be punishment, it is the sanction most frequently used by the courts to punish a criminal offender. Three out of every four criminals convicted of a crime in the United States are placed on probation (Glaze and Palla 2005). Nonetheless, America is heavily criticized, both at home and abroad, for the number of people it incarcerates (Currie 1998). Careful review of the failure rates and criminal activity of probationers nationwide, however, might cause some to argue that *more* criminals should go to prison, rather than fewer.

Although statistics on the failure rates and criminal activity of probationers are not centrally collected in the United States on a routine basis, in 1995, the Bureau of Justice Statistics released a report entitled *Probation and Parole Violators in State Prison, 1991* (Cohen, 1995). The purpose of the study was to determine how many of the inmates committed to prison were on probation or parole when they were incarcerated. The study's results do not reflect particularly positive outcomes. According to the report, there were a total of 459,337 criminals committed to state prisons in 1991; and 162,000 (35 percent) of them had been on probation at the time they were incarcerated. Seventy-four percent of the 162,000 had been convicted of committing a new crime. The remaining 26 percent had their probation revoked by the court for violating one or more of the conditions of their probation. Conditions of probation typically include abstaining from alcohol and drugs; avoiding contact or association with other criminals; maintaining gainful employment; and participating in specialized substance abuse, mental health, or sex offender treatment. Strikingly, a substantial number (87 percent) of those probationers who had violated a condition of their probation and were sent to prison in 1991 self-reported that although they had not been convicted of a new crime, they had been arrested for a new crime while on probation.

The average amount of time criminals spent on probation before committing a violation was seventeen months. About half of the probation violators had their probation terminated, and were sent to prison within one year of their release. During the average seventeen-month probationary period, the 162,000 probation violators had committed 44,000 violent crimes, 35,000 property crimes, 30,000 drug offenses, and 10,000 other offenses. More specifically, the 162,000 probationers had accounted for 6,400 murders, and the rapes or sexual assaults of 6,700 females and 700 males. One-third of the victims who had been raped or sexually assaulted were under the age of twelve, and two-thirds were under the age of eighteen. Seventeen thousand people had been robbed by a probationer, 10,400 people had been assaulted, 15,600 homes and businesses had been burglarized, and 3,100 motor vehicles had been stolen.

Using these statistics, supporters of the classical approach to crime prevention could argue that the failure rate of probationers and the serious nature of the crimes some of them commit suggest that more criminals, not less, should be sent to prison; and that fewer criminals, not more, should be placed on probation. As a matter of practice, the sanction imposed—probation or prison—may have little or nothing to do with which sanction more effectively prevents or deters criminal behavior. The primary reason probation is used more extensively than prison may be because it is less costly monetarily to supervise a criminal on probation than it is to keep him or her in prison. As the cost analysis presented in chapter 13 reveals, incarcerating the 4,151,121 criminals on probation in 2004 would have cost the taxpayers an average of more than 250 dollars a day if they were in prison.

Prison

A prison is generally classified as one of four types: super-maximum security, maximum security, medium security, or minimum security. In addition, many corrections systems also operate two other types of facilities: camps and halfway houses (also called transitional living centers) (Johnston 2002; Russell 1993).

Super-Maximum-Security Prisons

Super-maximum-security prisons are designed to house prisoners who have a long, established history of violent behavior, who pose a severe threat to the physical well-being of other inmates and prison personnel, and who would also pose a severe threat to the general public if they were to escape from confinement. Super-maximum-security prisons typically consist of a single building that is constructed of concrete reinforced with metal rebar. The perimeter of a super-maximum prison is secured by a concrete wall or two security fences. Armed guards are posted either in strategically positioned watch towers around the secure perimeter or in vehicles that patrol outside the secure perimeter. Inmates in a super-maximum security prison are confined to single-occupancy cells for twenty-three hours a day. The cell doors are made of solid-core metal and are equipped with a small viewing/pass-through window. The locks on the cell doors are electronically controlled from a remote, isolated location. Each cell is equipped with a bunk securely attached to the floor, a toilet, and a small hand-sink. Cell lights are secured behind wire-mesh grills and are controlled by prison personnel outside the cell. In a super-maximum security prison, prisoners are allowed out of their cells for one hour daily to exercise and shower, during which time they may be placed in handcuffs connected to a belly chain and leg irons. They are not permitted to work, participate in any self-improvement programs, or engage in any form of group activity. Meals are served to prisoners in their cells. Visits from family and friends are conducted in a cubicle equipped with an intercom and the inmate is separated from the visitor by a glass or Plexiglas partition. No physical contact between the visitor and the inmate is allowed.

Maximum-Security Prisons

Maximum-security prisons are designed to house prisoners who have exhibited aggressive behavior, but who have not established a pattern of violent behavior. Inmates in a maximum-security prison are considered a lesser threat to the health and well-being of other inmates, prison personnel, and the general public than those housed in super-maximum-security prisons. A maximum-security prison is often comprised of multiple buildings constructed of concrete reinforced with metal rebar. Perimeter security, cell house design and fixtures are essentially the same as those in a super-maximum security prison. Because inmates in a maximum-security prison are considered less of a risk than inmates in a super maximum security prison, they are permitted to engage in group activities and are allowed out of their cells daily to eat, work, exercise, shower, participate in self-improvement programs, attend religious services if they choose, and receive visits. Visits from family and friends are typically conducted in a large open room. Prisoners and their visitors may be prohibited from having any physical contact. If contact visits are allowed, the prisoner and visitor may be permitted to kiss and embrace at the beginning and end of the visiting period. Visitors are subject to physical searches at the beginning and end of a visiting period. Prisoners are searched prior to entering and upon leaving a visiting room. All movement and group activity is rigorously controlled, carefully supervised, and approved in advance.

Medium-Security Prisons

Medium-security prisons are designed to house prisoners who have no history of violent or aggressive behavior, and are considered a moderate threat to the health and well-being of other inmates, prison personnel, and the general public. A medium-security prison is often comprised of multiple buildings, which are typically constructed out of concrete reinforced with metal rebar, but may be constructed of materials that are less rigid and impenetrable than those used in the construction of a super-maximum or maximum-security prison. The perimeter of a medium-security prison is secured by a double security fence. Armed guards are posted either in strategically positioned watch towers around the secure perimeter or in vehicles that patrol outside the fence line. Housing accommodations in a medium-security prison may include a mixture of single-occupancy cells, multiple-occupancy cells, and multiple-occupancy dormitories. Dormitories resemble military barracks and are equipped with bunk beds stacked two high, foot-lockers for storage of clothing and personal property, group toilets, a shower area, and sinks. Inmates in a medium-security prison are allowed out of their living quarters daily to eat, work, exercise, shower, participate in self-improvement programs, attend religious services, and receive visits. Visits with family and friends are conducted in large open rooms, often equipped with tables, chairs, and vending machines. Prisoners and their visitors are normally allowed to kiss and embrace at the beginning and end of a visiting period. Visitors are subject to physical searches at the beginning and end of a visiting period. Prisoners are searched prior to entering and upon leaving a visiting room. All movement and group activity is supervised, but is less rigidly controlled than in the visiting rooms of higher-security prisons.

Minimum-Security Prisons

Minimum-security prisons are designed to house inmates who present no apparent threat to the life, health, or safety of other inmates or prison personnel and are not considered an escape risk, or a threat to the general public if they were to escape. A minimum-security prison may consist of a single building or several buildings, but usually fewer buildings than would be found in a medium- or maximum-security prison. The building(s) may be constructed of materials that might also be used to construct a commercial office or apartment building in the community. The perimeter of the property is typically not secured with a security fence; if it is, only a single fence is normally used. Unarmed guards conduct random patrols inside and outside the building(s). There are no watchtowers. Housing accommodations in a minimum-security prison are normally multiple-occupancy dormitories. These dormitories resemble military barracks and are equipped with bunk beds stacked two high, foot-lockers for storage of clothing and personal property, group toilets, a shower area, and sinks. In minimum-security prisons, inmates are allowed out of their living quarters daily to eat, work, exercise, shower, participate in self-improvement programs, attend religious services if they choose, and receive visits. Visits with family and friends may be permitted inside or outside the main building. Visitors and prisoners may embrace and kiss at the beginning and end of the visiting period. Prisoners may be allowed to hold their children during visits and to hold hands with their adult visitor if they wish. Visitors are subject to searches at the beginning and end of a visiting period. Prisoners will be searched prior to entering and upon leaving a visiting area. All movement and group activities are monitored, but not always supervised.

An in-depth discussion about the use of prisons in America's corrections system and their effectiveness is presented in chapter 12.

Camps

Traditional-style camps house low-risk inmates who perform a variety of public-works such as road repair, park maintenance, and forest restoration. Prisoners confined to these camps are normally serving a short-term sentence of eighteen months or less, and have no history of having been convicted of a violent crime or sex offense. These camps are generally located in remote rural locations. Living facilities are usually rustic, and consist of multi-occupancy cabins and one or more multipurpose buildings for showers, latrines, laundry, food service, religious services, indoor recreation, and visits.

In the early 1980s, the states of Georgia and Oklahoma instituted a new type of camp called a "boot camp." During the following ten years, thirty-six states and the federal government opened forty-seven boot camps for adult criminals. Styled after military basic-training programs, the operational philosophy of a boot camp emphasizes strict discipline, regimentation, strenuous physical conditioning, hard physical labor, and military-style drills. Some boot camps provide educational and counseling programs at night. Prisoners dress in military-type fatigues, march in formation to and from activities, and are prohibited from speaking unless spoken to by camp personnel. The typical offender assigned to a boot camp is a young (seventeen-to-twenty-five-year-old) first-time property offender.

The results of two follow-up evaluations indicate that the recidivism rate for prisoners who had been released from a boot camp after successfully completing the program is not significantly better than that of prisoners from the same age group and with comparable criminal histories that had been released from a traditional prison after serving a longer period of time. The evaluations did find, however, that the attitudes of boot camp participants toward their prison experience were more positive than the attitudes of those inmates who had been incarcerated in a traditional prison. As a group, boot camp inmates reported that they believed the boot camp experience to have changed them in a positive way, while inmates released from a traditional prison did not claim a similar benefit from their incarceration (MacKenzie 1994; Parent 2003).

Halfway Houses (Transitional Living Centers)

As the name implies, a halfway house (also known as a transitional living center) is used to house prisoners who are nearing completion of a prison term and are in the process of moving from a higher-level security prison to the community. A halfway house is typically a single building similar in design and construction to a college dormitory or military barracks, and is most often located in or near a metropolitan area. The exterior doors of the building are locked only at night to provide perimeter security. Unarmed personnel conduct random inspections inside the building and may conduct spot checks outside the building to ensure that all prisoners are accounted for. Prisoners in a halfway house are allowed to leave the facility at any time during the day or night to go to an approved job, to attend school, or to participate in other authorized community-based programs intended to help the prisoner make a successful transition from prison to the community. Visits with family and friends may be permitted inside or outside the main building. Visitors and prisoners may embrace and kiss at the beginning and end of the visiting period. Prisoners may be allowed to hold their children during the visit, and to hold hands with their adult visitor during the visit if they wish. Visitors are not routinely subject to physical searches at the beginning and end of a visiting period. Prisoners are randomly searched prior to entering and upon leaving a visiting area. All movement and group activities are monitored, but not always supervised.

A 1981 study, *Non-residential Work Release: A More Cost-Effective Approach to Transitional Programming,* concludes that the success rate of prisoners who are transitioned from prison to the community on temporary leave tend to do as well or better than prisoners who are transitioned through a halfway house. The study also concludes that the cost of the furlough approach is far less costly (Toombs 1981).

Capital Punishment

In stark contrast to most of Europe, Canada, and dozens of other countries throughout the world that have abolished or stringently restricted the use of capital punishment during the last quarter of the twentieth century, the legislative bodies of thirty-eight American states, as well as the United States Congress, have enacted laws that authorize its use. According to the Bureau of Justice Statistics, 820 criminals were executed by thirty-two states and the federal government between January 1977 (when the death penalty was reinstated in the United States) and December 31, 2002. Two-thirds of the executions occurred in five states: Texas (289), Virginia (87), Missouri (59), Oklahoma (55), and Florida (54). As of January 31, 2002, there were 3,447 convicted murderers awaiting execution in the prisons of thirty-eight states and the federal government (Bonczar and Snell 2003).

While there is little debate about whether capital punishment is the ultimate form of punishment (some argue that a life sentence without possibility of parole is as punitive, if not more punitive—see Bedau 19977) there is seemingly no end to other arguments surrounding this controversial practice. Chief among the topics that continue to be debated are the legality of capital punishment, its effectiveness as a deterrent, its morality, and its potential discriminatory nature.

The Legality of Capital Punishment

In the United States, most challenges to the legality of capital punishment have been based primarily on the argument that capital punishment is a cruel and unusual form of punishment, and as such violates the Eighth Amendment to the Constitution, which forbids the use of cruel and unusual punishment. Legal challenges have also been directed at the method used for execution, based on the argument that the pain inflicted by a particular method is cruel and unusual.

> Excessive bail shall not be required, nor excessive fines imposed, nor cruel and unusual punishment inflicted. (Eighth Amendment, U.S. Constitution)

Opponents also argue that the death penalty denies defendants equal protection under the law, which is guaranteed by the Fourteenth Amendment.

> No State shall make or enforce any law which shall abridge the privileges or immunities of citizens of the United States; nor shall any State deprive any person of life, liberty, or property without due process of law; nor deny any person within its jurisdiction the equal protection of the laws. (Fourteenth Amendment, U. S. Constitution)

Although the Supreme Court has never ruled that the death penalty violates either the Eighth or Fourteenth Amendment of the Constitution, the court did rule in 1972 that the death penalty is unconstitutional if the sentencing procedures use to impose the penalty do not make adequate provisions to prevent the arbitrary and capricious imposition of the penalty (Furman v. Georgia 408 U. S.

238). The Court reaffirmed this decision in 1976 when it ruled the sentencing procedures used to impose the death penalty on Troy Gregg were sufficient to ensure the sentence was neither arbitrary nor capricious (Gregg v. Georgia 428 U. S. 153). The Supreme Court has upheld the use of hanging, firing squad, electric chair, and gas chamber. A decision regarding the use of lethal injection, which is currently the preferred method of execution, has not yet been ruled upon by the high Court.

Until another case is filed challenging the constitutionality of the death penalty and the Supreme Court agrees to review the case, or until the Constitution is amended, capital punishment is legal in the United States.

The Morality of Capital Punishment

The rationale for the argument of those who oppose capital punishment on moral grounds is that intentionally taking a human being's life is immoral, whether the person is murdered by another human being or executed by the government. Opponents argue that both a murder and an execution are acts born out of hate, vengeance, anger, and resentment. The government, opponents say, should not knowingly engage in such behavior because by doing so, it in effect shows the same disregard for human life as does a murderer. In practicing capital punishment, a government symbolically condones killing, rather than conveying its rejection of the behavior (Bedau 1997).

Those who support capital punishment typically justify it morally by: 1) differentiating between a murder and an execution; 2) classifying an execution as an act of justified retribution rather than revenge; and 3) citing the results of studies that refute the allegation that capital punishment discriminates against minorities. According to those who support capital punishment, murder is usually statutorily defined as the unlawful, malicious, or premeditated killing of one human being by another. An execution, therefore, does not meet this definition of murder because an execution is a lawful action taken without malice by the government, not by an individual. An execution is understood as retribution, which differs from malice, retaliation, or revenge, according to capital punishment supporters, in several critical ways. First, retribution is taken in response to an established wrong. Actions taken in revenge or as retaliation are driven by a perceived wrong. Second, retribution is governed by strict limits, which have been established to ensure that the degree of punishment imposed is suitable to the crime. Actions taken in revenge, out of malice, or in retaliation have no boundaries to limit the extent or degree of punishment. Third, retribution is an impartial act taken to protect the interests of society as a whole, not for personal satisfaction, which latter is the motivation for actions taken in revenge, out of malice, or in retaliation (Cassell 2004; Judd 2003).

> Society has a right to protect itself from capital offenses even if this means taking a finite chance of executing an innocent person.
>
> Fire trucks occasionally kill innocent pedestrians while racing to fires, but we accept these losses as justified by the greater good of the activity of using fire trucks. We judge the use of automobiles to be acceptable even though such use causes an average 50,000 traffic fatalities each year. We accept the morality of a defensive war even though it will result in our troop's accidentally or mistakenly killing innocent people.
>
> That an occasional error may be made, regrettable though this is, is not a sufficient reason for us to refuse to use the death penalty, if on balance it serves a just and useful function. (Pojman 2004, p. 68)

The debate about whether capital punishment is moral or immoral is essentially a philosophical argument. There is no court of last resort to decide this question as the

Supreme Court can with the question of legality. There is no scientific evidence upon which a final answer can be based that is not subject to intense debate. The answer is dependent on the personal philosophy of each individual or group.

The Deterrent Effect of Capital Punishment

The debate about whether the death penalty is an effective deterrent centers on the question of whether or not executing one criminal for murder deters others from committing murder. There is no question that the criminal who is executed will never commit another crime of any type; but will others be dissuaded from committing similar crimes out of fear that they too will be executed if they are caught and convicted?

Isaac Ehrlich, currently chairman of the economics department at the University of Buffalo in New York State, was one of the first scholars to use statistical methods to calculate the effect of capital punishment on murder rates. Using the techniques of cost-benefit analysis, Ehrlich constructed an economic model of analysis based on two basic propositions about murder and other crimes against persons. The first proposition stated that murder and other crimes against persons are committed largely as a result of hate, jealousy, and other interpersonal conflicts involving pecuniary and non-pecuniary motives, or as a by-product of crimes against property. The second proposition stated that one's propensity to perpetrate such crimes is influenced by the prospective gains and losses associated with their commission. Applying his economic model and a parade of statistical methods, Ehrlich analyzed aggregate crime data regarding murder and capital punishment and came to the conclusion that "law enforcement activities in general and executions in particular do exert a deterrent effect on acts of murder" (Ehrlich 1975, p. 416).

In a separate study conducted by the economics department at the University of Colorado, researchers reported that they found a statistically significant relationship between executions, pardons, and homicide rates. Specifically, they concluded that every execution prevents five or six additional homicides. Conversely, they claimed that pardons or commutations of death sentences result, statistically speaking, in the commission of 1.5 to 2 additional murders.

According to the standard economic model of crime, a rational offender would respond to perceived costs and benefits of committing crime. Capital punishment is particularly significant in this context, because it represents a very high cost for committing murder (loss of life). Thus the presence of capital punishment in a state, or the frequency with which it is used, should unequivocally deter homicide. (Mocan and Gittings 2001, p.1)

The results of yet a third study conducted by members of the faculty of the economics department at Emory University support the findings reported by the University of Colorado. Researchers at Emory University examined the death sentences imposed in the United States from 1977 through 1996 (nearly 6000 cases) and compared changes in homicide rates in over 3000 counties nationwide to the likelihood of being executed in each county. The results of this study, say its authors, suggest that capital punishment has a strong deterrent effect. Any increase in arrest, sentencing, or execution tends to reduce the murder rates. The study concludes that each execution, on average, results in eighteen fewer murders (Dezhbakhsh, Rubin, and Shepard 2003).

In spite of the sense of certainty attached to these conclusions, not all researchers are persuaded. Richard Berk, professor of statistics at the University of California in Los Angeles (UCLA) and author of *New Claims about Executions and General Deterrence: Déjà vu All Over Again*, asserts that the data analysis used to support such claims are flawed, containing significant statistical errors caused by the problem of "influence," which occurs when a very small and atypical fraction of the available data dominates the statistical results of a study.

After reanalyzing the data used in the Mocan/Gittings study as well as other studies, Berk found that the key explanatory variable used in these studies was the number of executions by state and year; but because most states in most years execute no one and only a very few states execute more than five people in any given year, the sample size is too small to draw any generalized conclusions.

> The results raise serious questions about whether anything useful about the deterrent value of the death penalty can ever be learned from an observational study with the data that are likely to be available. With an intervention that is so highly skewed, a very small portion of the data will likely impart significant influence on the results. (Berk 2004, p.24)

One method used by opponents of capital punishment to measure its effectiveness as a deterrent is to compare the murder rates of the twelve states that do not allow capital punishment (Alaska, Hawaii, Iowa, Maine, Massachusetts,

Michigan, Minnesota, North Dakota, Rhode Island, Vermont, West Virginia, and Wisconsin) with those of the thirty-eight states that do permit it. The table below, developed by the Death Penalty Information Center, reflects the comparative murder rates from 1990 to 2002 for states with the death penalty and states without the death penalty.

Table 5: Murder Rates

Year	Murder Rate in States With Death Penalty	Murder Rate in States Without Death Penalty
1990	9.50	9.16
1991	9.94	9.27
1992	9.51	8.63
1993	9.69	8.81
1994	9.23	7.88
1995	8.59	6.78
1996	7.72	5.37
1997	7.09	5.00
1998	6.51	4.61
1999	5.86	4.59
2000	5.70	4.25
2001	5.87	4.25
2002	5.82	4.27

Those who argue that capital punishment is not a deterrent also offer comparisons between the homicide rate of the United States and those of foreign countries that do not permit capital punishment. Data included in a report published by the British Home Office in October 2003 indicate that the murder rate of the United States (6.36 per

100,000) is more than three times the rate of Sweden (1.94 per 100,000), the Netherlands (1.66 per 100,000), France (1.63 per 100,000), Italy (1.56 per 100,000), Great Britain (1.45 per 100,000), and Germany (1.28 per 100,000)—all countries in which capital punishment is prohibited. Data released by the Canadian government in December 2001 indicate that the homicide rate of Canada—another country that prohibits capital punishment—is, at 1.80 per 100,000, also three times smaller than that of the United States.

The logic that supports the argument that capital punishment is an effective deterrent is the same logic which supports the classical school of correctional thought generally—that criminal behavior is the result of a series of conscious acts that can be influenced. If potential murderers knew for certain they would be executed for killing another human being, the murder would not be committed. Opponents of the death penalty support their argument with the opposite view: most crimes, and particularly murder, are impulsive, unplanned acts; and even in those instances where the crime has been planned, the criminal is undeterred by the threat of punishment because the criminal either thinks he or she will not be caught or doesn't care if he or she is caught. The argument over the deterrent effect of the death penalty, like so many other aspects of the debate over what causes criminal behavior and how to prevent it, is based more on mythical notions and intuitive beliefs than measurable results.

Discriminatory Effect of Capital Punishment

Some opponents of the death penalty assert that racial minorities, particularly blacks and Hispanics, are more likely to be arrested, convicted, and executed for committing a capital crime than are whites (Bedau and Radelet 1987; Radelet et al. 1992; Huff et al. 1996; Westervelt and Humphrey 2001; and Parker et al. 2003). This assertion is based primarily on the analysis and interpretation of the demographic data (regarding gender, race, education level, and age) collected by the Department of Justice in relation to all persons sentenced to death or executed in the United States since 1977; as well as on independent studies focused on specific factors such as the race of persons exonerated by new evidence after being convicted of a capital offense (Scheck 2000). Proponents of the death penalty dispute the assertion that capital punishment is discriminatory by challenging the validity and veracity of the opponents' data analysis, interpretation, and independent studies, and by presenting their own (Cassell, 2004; Sampson and Lauritsen 1997; Wilbanks 1987; and

Langan 1976). As a result, the question of whether capital punishment racially discriminates remains open to debate.

Readers interested in a more comprehensive discussion of the issues surrounding the debate about capital punishment might wish to contact the following organizations. Some of the organizations advocating capital punishment are the Criminal Justice Legal Foundation, Justice for All, and Pro Death Penalty. A few of the organizations opposing capital punishment are the Death Penalty Information Center, Amnesty International, and the American Civil Liberties Union. For the most recent data collected by the Department of Justice, see the *Bureau of Justice Bulletin: Capital Punishment.*

Chapter 3

THE AMERICAN JUSTICE SYSTEM: SWIFT AND CERTAIN?

The U.S. Bureau of Justice Statistics estimates that there were a total of 11,695,264 crimes reported in 2004—10,328,255 property crimes and 1,367,009 violent crimes. Only 16.5 percent of the property crimes and 43.7 percent of the violent crimes were cleared by arrest or exceptional means, which as was discussed earlier means some force outside the agency's control prevented the arrest of the individual. Based on these rates, a criminal has a better than 50 percent chance of avoiding arrest for a violent crime and a better than 80 percent chance of avoiding arrest for a property crime (Federal Bureau of Investigation 2005). These numbers suggest that most criminals are never caught, which makes punishment highly uncertain.

Every two years, the United States Department of Justice collects sentencing information from approximately 300 of the nation's 3000 plus counties. At least one county is selected from each of the 50 states. The data collected is compiled by the Bureau of Justice Statistics into detailed information about state sentencing practices, which is published in a bulletin titled *Felony Sentences in State Courts*. The most recent bulletin, published in December 2004, contains data collected for the year 2002. This bulletin indicates that the median time (the median being the point below and above which 50 percent of all cases fall) from arrest to sentencing for an estimated 1,114,217 adult offenders convicted of a felony was about six months. Absent a universal definition of swiftness, no general conclusion can be made as to whether a six-month delay from the time of arrest to the time of sentencing can be considered swift, but common sense would suggest that it cannot (Durose and Langan 2004).

The American justice system presumes that a person is innocent until proven guilty. This system is, by design, a deliberate and methodical process that is neither swift nor certain. But perhaps it is not the amount of time that elapses between arrest and sentencing that is of critical importance for punishment to be an effective deterrent against criminal behavior. Perhaps it is instead, the amount of time that elapses from the moment a person first demonstrates a propensity for criminal behavior, until punishment is imposed, that is of critical importance.

Currently, the typical response to delinquent behavior in youth is counseling. If this proves ineffective and the individual continues to display chronic delinquent tendencies, he or she is sent to a training school or reformatory—not as punishment, but to be retrained and reformed. It is not until a criminal offender reaches the chronological age of adulthood or is remanded to adult court because of a crime's severity that punishment is imposed as a sanction. If it is the amount of time that elapses from the moment a person first demonstrates a propensity for criminal behavior until punishment is imposed that is critical for punishment to be effective, it could be argued that the use of punishment as a sanction to deter criminal behavior needs to be applied as soon as criminal behavior manifests itself, not after the behavior has become habitual.

What is the likelihood that the use of punishment as a sanction by the criminal justice system will be applied sooner rather than later? A recent case in the state of Florida involving the murder of a six-year-old child by a twelve-year-old boy, and a January 2004 Supreme Court ruling offer some insight. In 1999, a twelve-year-old boy killed a six-year-old girl by body-slamming her to the floor and striking her with assorted kicks and punches—techniques he reportedly told authorities he had learned from watching professional wrestling on television. After his mother, a Florida State Highway Patrol trooper, turned down a plea bargain for three years in prison for manslaughter, the boy was tried and convicted of first-degree murder and sentenced to life in prison. In 2003, the Florida Appellate Court overturned the conviction and life sentence on the grounds that the boy's mental competency was not taken into proper consideration at the time of the original trial. Rather than retry the boy, who was then seventeen, the prosecutor offered and the boy's mother accepted the same plea agreement that she had turned down earlier. As provided in the plea agreement, the boy was sentenced to three years in prison with credit for time served, one year of house arrest, and ten years of probation. This resulted in his immediate release from custody. Unfortunately, this youthful offender failed to profit from the court's leniency. In September 2004, the court extended his probation to 15 years after the boy was found by police to be in possession of a knife outside his house. In May 2005, the boy's probation was revoked, and he was returned to jail, where he awaited prosecution on charges of armed robbery and burglary with battery after a pizza deliveryman identified him as the person who had robbed him at gunpoint. In May 2006, the now nineteen-year-old was sentenced to thirty years in prison (CNN 2004; CNN 2005; CNN 2006).

Prior to March 2005, the laws of fourteen states allowed sixteen-year-old offenders to be executed for murder, and the laws of five additional states permitted the execution of seventeen-year-olds convicted of murder. In March 2005, the United States Supreme Court ruled, in a five to four decision, that the Eighth Amendment of the Constitution, which bans cruel and unusual forms of punishment, prohibits the execution of any offender who was under eighteen years of age when a crime was committed (*Roper v. Simmons*). The Court's decision overruled a contrary Supreme Court decision made in 1989 (in *Stanford v. Kentucky*) that had upheld the constitutionality of executing youthful offenders.

Justice Anthony Kennedy, writing in support of the 2005 ruling, justified the majority opinion in part by pointing out that not only do most American states prohibit the execution of juvenile offenders, but that "[t]he United States is the only country in the world that continues to give official sanction to the juvenile death penalty." Justice Sandra Day O'Connor, writing in dissent of the ruling, argued that although the Court had found support for its decision in the fact that a majority of states disallow capital punishment of seventeen-year-old offenders, it cannot be asserted that its decision had been compelled by a genuine national consensus.

The results of the Florida case and the divergence of opinion among the justices of the Supreme Court both reflect the ambivalence in thought and practice held by

American society regarding the use of punishment to deter and prevent criminal behavior among young people. This ambivalence suggests that change in the practice of deferring the use of punishment as a sanction until criminals reach adulthood is unlikely; and this lack of change makes it impossible to rigorously test the validity of the idea that punishment can deter and prevent criminal behavior if it is applied swiftly and with certainty.

Section 1 of Article 14 of the United States Constitution states: "All persons born or naturalized in the United States and subject to the jurisdiction thereof, are citizens of the United States and the state wherein they reside. No state shall make or enforce any law which shall abridge the privileges or immunities of citizens of the United States; nor shall any state deprive any person of life, liberty, or property, without due process of law; nor deny to any person within its jurisdiction the equal protection of the laws."

Some unwavering advocates of punishment argue that the way to make it a more effective deterrent to crime is to streamline the court process to ensure that punishment is delivered more expeditiously. Others argue that punishment is not an effective deterrent because prison life is not harsh enough. Criminals have more rights than victims, say these critics (Crawford and Gooley eds. 2000).

For purposes of this discussion, the operative words in the Constitution are *all persons born or naturalized are citizens and no state shall make or enforce any law which shall abridge the privileges or immunities of citizens, deprive any person of life, liberty, property, or equal protection of the law, without benefit of due process.* The Constitution does not say that all persons *except criminals* are citizens, or that criminals forfeit any constitutional right when they are convicted and sentenced. The judicial process cannot be streamlined to expedite due process, and prison conditions cannot be made harsher unless Article 14 of the Constitution is removed or amended to redefine the due process provisions and to restrict the constitutional rights of criminals, or to declare them constitutionally dead. Given the intensity of feeling that staunch pro-punishment advocates have about this issue, it is surprising that an organized effort to amend the Constitution has not yet been mounted.

The belief that criminals should be punished for their crimes is understandable, but it is questionable whether inflicting punishment will permanently alter a criminal's behavior or deter others from committing a crime. Critics of the punishment model argue that fear is the same catalyst that has been used unsuccessfully to persuade people to stop smoking or drinking and driving, and that it is no more successful at preventing crime. Punishment opponents point out that in some Islamic states, where torture, physical abuse, physical dismemberment, stoning, and other grotesque forms of execution are regularly practiced, fear has failed to prevent citizens from committing criminal acts or engaging in violent acts of civil disobedience.

Although the fear induced by punishment or the threat of punishment may sometimes produce the desired results, the degree of punishment and the severity of the threat required to force change in a person's behavior vary dramatically from one person to another, and the changes are typically temporary. When punishment is discontinued or its threat removed, the behavioral changes induced in the person being punished or threatened often dissipate, and the person reverts to the behavioral patterns that had predominated before he or she was subjected to punishment or the threat of punishment. Marvin Marshall, one of the world's foremost authorities on the use of intrinsic motivation to foster individual and social responsibility, says in his most recent book, *Discipline Without Stress, Punishments, or Rewards: How Teachers and Parents Promote Responsibility and Learning,* that the effects of punishment are temporary and transitory. Punishment may force compliance, but it does not change behavior (Marshall 2002).

Part 2

The Positivist School

Chapter 4

HISTORICAL FOUNDATION AND THEORETICAL OVERVIEW

The thinking and beliefs of the classical school went essentially unchallenged until the essays of Auguste Comte were published in the mid-eighteenth and early nineteenth centuries. Comte was a French philosopher who is considered by some to have been the father of modern sociology. He theorized that human intelligence passes through three stages: the theological, the metaphysical, and the scientific or positive stages. In the theological stage human intelligence seeks to account for the world by seeing it as under the control of supernatural beings. In the metaphysical stage, human intelligence seeks an explanation for mysterious abstract forces (e.g., nature). In the scientific or positive stage, the focus of human intelligence is on discovering the empirical relationships between different phenomena. Comte's objective was to make sociology a science—like astronomy, physics, or chemistry—so that social problems could be solved objectively. According to Comte, examining social problems with a positivist philosophy shows that while certain wrongs are inevitable and others are curable, it is foolish to try to cure the incurable in social as well as in biological and chemical matters. It was the thinking of Comte that led to development of the positivist school theories in the field of corrections (Thompson 1976; Harp 1995).

The philosophy of the positivist school is diametrically opposed to that of the classical school. Positivist school theorists believe that criminal behavior is a product of factors over which the criminal has no control, and not the product of free will as the classical school theorists proclaim. There is, however, no consensus within the positivist school about what underlying, uncontrollable factors precipitate criminal behavior. Some students of the positivist school argue that criminal behavior is caused by biological factors—criminals are simply born with criminal tendencies. Others insist that criminal behavior is the result of exposure to negative psychological or sociological factors in one's environment, over which he or she has no control.

Chapter 5

BIOLOGICAL DETERMINISM

"Criminals are born, not made," is the claim of those who believe that biological factors produce criminal behavior. But exactly how criminals differ biologically from non-criminals, and whether the biological anomalies are random mutations, genetic flaws that are passed along from one generation to another or selected genes that are acquired and passed along, is a matter of conjecture and debate within this group.

Bodily Fluids[2]

The origin of the idea that behavioral differences between people are attributable to inherent differences in physiological makeup can be traced back to the theories of Hippocrates. A Greek physician born in 460 BC, Hippocrates is known today as the "Father of Medicine,"

---

2   See Item 1in the Addendum for a discussion about DNA analysis, a process involving the analysis of bodily fluids that has thus far been of no use in the search for the cause(s) of criminal behavior; but has proved to be of great value in aiding with the determination of an accused person's guilt or innocence.

and as the author of the Hippocratic Oath to which all physicians swear allegiance. Hippocrates postulated that all humans possess four bodily fluids called humors—yellow bile, black bile, blood, and phlegm—in varying amounts. The relative concentrations in the body of the four humors result, according to the theory, in two different pairs of body qualities—warm versus cool and dry versus moist. The relative balance among these body qualities, says Hippocrates, is what produces variations in behavior between people (Jones 1931).

Hippocrates' explanation for individual differences in behavior remained the standard until the second century AD, when Claudius Galen, another Greek physician and considered by many to be the next most important contributor to classical medicine after Hippocrates, expanded on his predecessor's thinking. According to Galen, a person's temperament fits into one of four categories: melancholic, sanguine, choleric, or phlegmatic. The melancholic temperament, which characteristically involves sadness or depression, is caused by an excess of black bile. The sanguine temperament, which describes one who is warm and pleasant, is caused by excess blood. The choleric temperament, which is fiery and hot-tempered, is caused by excess yellow bile. The phlegmatic temperament, categorizing one who is apathetic and slovenly, is caused by too much phlegm (Kagen 1994).

Physiognomy

Giambattista della Porta, a fourteenth-century Italian physician, first proposed the concept of physiognomy. According to Giambattista, a person's character could be discovered by interpreting his or her outward appearance—especially the features of the face—rather than by measuring the relative balance of the four humors. For example, large, protruding facial features—particularly the nose, lips, and jaw—were all suggested to be indicators of a criminal character (Glubb 1965).

Phrenology

In the early nineteenth century, Franz Gall, a Viennese physician, proposed the concept of phrenology. The basic premise of phrenology is that an individual's brain is comprised of multiple distinct areas that determine an individual's personality, intellect, disposition, and aptitudes, among other things. Gall claimed that as the skull forms over the brain, the shape and size of each area in the brain creates indentations and bumps on the outer surface of the skull. By running one's fingers and palms over the skull, one could supposedly interpret the bumps and the indentations, thus revealing an individual's personality, disposition, character, psychological traits, and intellectual aptitudes (Van Wyne 2003; Sabbatini 1997).

Atavism

In the late nineteenth century, Cesare Lombroso, an Italian psychiatrist who had been strongly influenced by Darwin's theory of evolution, proposed that criminals were an "atavism" in the evolutionary chain, meaning that criminals were a throwback to a lower form of life with physical features and social traits similar to those of apes. Physically, Lombroso observed, criminals typically have long arms, large ears, flat noses, fat lips, high cheekbones, strongly defined canine teeth, protruding jaws, extraordinary strength, and better-than-average agility. Socially, according to Lombroso, criminals manifest the behavior of a savage animal, and lack the ability to restrain or control their behavior (Gibson 2002). Although Lombroso acknowledged that some crimes were committed out of rage, passion, or desperation, he argued that "to understand crime one must study the criminal, not his rearing, not his education, not the current predicament that might have inspired his theft and pillage" (Reprint, p.126 in Gould's *The Mismeasure of Man*).

In an attempt to legitimize his theory, Lombroso documented massive amounts of statistical data, which he used to manufacture self-serving mathematical formulas designed to justify his positions. After undergoing intense scrutiny by the likes of Paul Broca and Paul Topinard—two French physicians who were pioneers in the fields of anthropology and neurology—Lombroso and his supposed discoveries eventually lost all credibility.

Somatotyping/Body Typing

In the early twentieth century, German psychiatrist Ernst Kretschmer offered yet another biological theory, which he called somatotyping or body typing. Later expanded upon by American psychologist William Sheldon, and Eleanor and Sheldon Glueck of the Harvard Law faculty, somatotyping is similar to physiognomy and phrenology in that it is more a method of identifying criminals than a means of explaining the etiology of criminal behavior or of preventing criminal behavior. According to Kretschmer, Sheldon, and the Gluecks, all human beings have one of three body types. Kretschmer labeled them asthenic, athletic, and pyknic. The Gluecks used the terms endomorphic, mesomorphic, and ectomorphic. Each of these body types was associated with a different mental disorder or behavioral pattern.

It was the view of Kretschmer, Sheldon, and the Gluecks that criminals have an athletic or mesomorphic body type (Arraji 1994; Glueck 1956; Kretschmer 1949). The asthenic or endomorphic body type is characterized by wide hips, narrow shoulders, large wrists and ankles, and excessive fat on the body, upper arms, and thighs. The athletic or mesomorphic body type is characterized by broad shoulders and narrow hips, a muscular body, very little fat, and strong forearms, calves, and thighs. The pyknic or ectomorphic body type is characterized by narrow shoulders, hips, and chest, a thin face, a high forehead, very little muscle or fat, and thin legs and arms.

Like those who continued to believe that the earth was flat when they were confronted with evidence to the contrary, there are still people in the twenty-first century who believe that physical traits are predictors of criminal behavior. As ridiculous as it seems, computer software programs and instructional kits for physiognomy and phrenology are now sold over the Internet.

Improper Diet or Vitamin Deficiency

Improper diet or vitamin deficiency is another theory that attempts to link criminal behavior to biological factors. Those who promote this concept have identified a number of food products which they claim are directly linked to criminal behavior. Others have argued there is evidence to suggest there is a strong link between deficiencies in vitamins and minerals and criminal behavior. In addition to the elimination of certain foods from the diet—specifically, foods containing refined sugar or white flour, foods with a high caloric content, dairy products, and citrus fruits—other suggested nutritional remedies include measured doses of vitamins, minerals, and special health foods. Most common among the recommended vitamins and minerals are niacin, pantothenic acid, thiamine, vitamin B6, folate, vitamin C, iron, magnesium, and amino acids of all sorts.

In 1988, the National Institute of Corrections commissioned the Rand Corporation to survey the literature on the most prominent behavioral science and nutrition studies that had been designed to explore the relationship between diet and criminal behavior. The studies reviewed included both those that had concluded that diet does significantly influence behavior, and those that concluded that diet does not have a significant effect on behavior. The authors of the report, titled *The Effects of Diet on Behavior: Implications for Criminology and Corrections*, were Diana Fishbein and Susan Pease. Fishbein and Pease concluded that because the studies had not been conducted in accordance with the fundamental principles of scientific investigation none of the studies they reviewed had produced sufficient empirical evidence to either support or refute the argument that diet has a significant impact on behavior.

In 2002, the *British Journal of Psychiatry* published the results of an eighteen-month study designed and conducted by Oxford University scientist C. Benard Gesch to specifically assess the influence of supplementary vitamins, minerals, and essential fatty acids on the antisocial behavior of young adult prisoners. The experiment was a double-blind, placebo-controlled, trial involving 231 randomly selected prisoners in a maximum-security prison in England. The aim of the experiment was to test the effects of diet supplements containing vitamins, minerals, and essential fatty acids on prisoner behavior by comparing the disciplinary records of the participating prisoners before, after, and during the test period.

Half of the study group was randomly selected to unknowingly receive the diet supplement, and the other half unknowingly received the placebo. When the results for each group were compared, the group taking the dietary supplements received an average of 26.3 percent fewer misconduct reports than the group taking the placebo. When compared to their baseline data, the results showed that the group taking the dietary supplements committed 35.1 percent fewer conduct violations, while the rate of misconduct for the placebo group remained virtually unchanged. Gesch and his colleagues readily admit that the results of their research are correlative only and, advise others not to make any generalized conclusions about criminal behavior on the basis of their findings.

Brain Disorders

Although the map of the brain created by the phrenologist Franz Gall had been incorrect, modern advancements in neurological science—particularly the use of computerized x-ray technology—has confirmed the general principle established by Gall that many bodily functions and physical abilities are indeed controlled by specific regions of the brain.[3] Researchers exploring the theory that brain disorders cause criminal behavior are currently examining two different causative factors: structural abnormality and chemical imbalance (Zawidski and Bechtel 2004).

---

3   See Item 2 in the Addendum for a description of "brain fingerprinting," a procedure that—like DNA analysis—is of no help determining what causes criminal behavior or how to prevent it, but may have potential for improving the process of determining if a suspect should even be charged with a crime.

Structural Abnormality

The development of new electromagnetic and digital imaging devices and techniques has created a more reliable and graphic method for investigators to explore the structure of the brain and to determine with more certainty how it works.

Using these techniques, medical science has determined that the brain is comprised of four distinct sections—the brain stem, the midbrain or cerebellum, the limbic system, and the cerebral cortex—and that each of these sections controls different bodily functions and physical and mental abilities. The brain stem controls the body's most basic and essential functions, such as heart rate, blood pressure, and temperature. The midbrain or cerebellum is responsible for controlling appetite and sleep. The limbic system controls emotions, such as pleasure, joy, anger, sadness, and remorse. The cerebral cortex is subdivided into four lobes: the occipital lobe, which controls vision; the parietal lobe, which controls the sense of touch and spatial understanding; the temporal lobe, which controls hearing and language; and the frontal lobe, which regulates body movement, planning, reasoning, memory, self-control, attention, and judgment (DSQUIC 2000).

As scientists have learned more about how the brain works, they have also gained insight into how a specific bodily function or behavior is affected when the area in the brain that is responsible for controlling it is rendered dysfunctional through injury, illness, or incomplete or incorrect development at birth. In terms of behavior, recent studies have led investigators to conclude that there may be a relationship between criminal behavior—particularly violent behavior—and structural abnormalities in the prefrontal cortex and the medial temporal lobes, which are the areas of the brain thought to be responsible for impulse-control, judgment, planning, remorse, concern for others, and concern for the consequences of one's actions (Bufkin and Luttrell 2005; and Raine et al. 2000). A coalition of medical researchers in Los Angles and San Francisco who have observed and compared the behavior of Alzheimer patients with that of other patients known to have prefrontal cortex damage, have found that both groups manifested unacceptable behavior that is characteristic of sociopaths—such as unsolicited sexual acts, physical assaults, and lack of remorse. The sociopathic type of personality or character is that which is most common among criminals (Mendez et al. 2005).

Chemical Imbalances

The theory that criminal behavior can be caused by an imbalance of the chemicals within the brain could be characterized as a modern-day version of Hippocrates' and Galen's theories. The difference is that Hippocrates and Galen attributed behavioral differences to the relative balance of blood, bile, and phlegm in the body, rather than to the balance of brain chemicals that had been unknown at the time.

Proponents of the chemical imbalance theory claim to have identified over fifty relevant chemical substances in the brain, which have been named neurotransmitters. The function of a neurotransmitter is to transmit messages between components of the brain, as well as messages from the brain to other parts of the body. The type and level of neurotransmitters in any given brain ostensibly determine both the message that is communicated, as well as this message's intensity. In theory, maintaining a proper balance of chemicals in the brain can prevent problematic behavior; just as regulating other chemicals and substances elsewhere in the body can prevent or control high blood pressure, high cholesterol, or diabetes. Four of the fifty chemicals— dopamine, serotonin, norepinephrine, and gamma-aminobutyric acid (GABA)—have been singled out by neurological researchers as being related to schizophrenia, depression, manic-depression, obsessive-compulsive, and attention-deficit hyperactivity disorder. GABA is a neurotransmitter inhibitor that discourages or blocks communication between cells in areas of the brain that control emotion and anxiety. Low levels of GABA, some researchers claim, cause impulse-control difficulty, which is one of the hallmark characteristics of criminal behavior (Carver 2002; Walsh 1994; Walsh 1988).

Researchers have also explored the role of an enzyme called monoamine oxidase, or MAOA, and have discovered that one of the functions MAOA serves is to neutralize the effects of serotonin after the serotonin is released by the brain in response to stress. A joint study on this subject was conducted by researchers from the Institute of Psychiatry at King's College in London, the Department of Psychology at the University of Wisconsin in Madison, and the Dunedin School of Medicine at the University of Otago in New Zealand. The results, released in 2002, suggest that the level of MAOA may be a determining factor in whether a person subjected to abuse or maltreatment as a child is at greater risk of developing a conduct disorder, demonstrating antisocial symptoms, or becoming a violent offender. After analyzing information about 442 adult males who had been monitored since their birth in 1972 and 1973, the researchers found that 154 of the men in this group had been abused or mistreated during the first ten years of their lives, and that 33 of the 154 had been severely mistreated. Abuse or mistreatment was defined as maternal rejection, frequent changes of the primary caregiver, physical abuse resulting in injury, and sexual abuse. The study reports that 85 percent of those who were severely mistreated as children that developed patterns of antisocial behavior had low levels of MAOA, while those members of the cohort who had high levels of MAOA rarely exhibited aggressive or criminal behavior in adulthood, even though they, too, had been severely abused as children (Avshalom et al. 2002).

Critics of the chemical imbalance theory charge that the theory is totally hypothetical and without scientific foundation because no one knows what the proper balance of chemicals in the brain should be, and because there is no proven scientific procedure that can be used to measure chemical levels in the brain. The popularity of the chemical imbalance theory is attributed by researchers at the Eaton T. Fores Research Center to an unholy alliance between drug companies and unscrupulous researchers. The drug companies, claim the critics, fund and promote the research into and profit from the sale of the drugs, which are distributed to the consumer by mental health practitioners who prescribe the medication who then credit the drug for the resulting change in behavior, a change that they had predicted in advance (Fores 2003; Lehmann 2002; Ashton 2001; Breggin and Cohen 1999).

There is no question that since psychotropic drugs became the treatment of choice within the mental health community; there has been a dramatic reduction in both the number of inpatient hospital facilities and the number of patients receiving mental health treatment in hospitals. Between 1955 and 1996, the number of people residing in institutions for the mentally ill declined from over 500,000 to 62,000. Much of the credit for this reduction has been attributed to the advent of pharmaceutical intervention, which has allowed for many institutions to be closed and for treatment of former inpatients to be provided in community mental health clinics. In contrast, the total number of criminals incarcerated in federal and state prisons and local jails increased from 744,208 in 1985 to 2,033,331 in 2002. While the population of institutionalized mentally ill people has dramatically decreased and the number of criminals incarcerated has dramatically increased, what may be of more significance is that the number of incarcerated criminals who are mentally ill has also dramatically increased—by as much as 14 percent, according to some estimates (Raphael 2000).

It could be argued that the reported improvements in patients that are commonly ascribed to chemical interventions are more a product of the Hawthorne Effect than of the medication. The Hawthorne Effect is an expected experimental effect resulting from the research participants having prior knowledge about the subject of research and, more importantly, having prior knowledge about what outcomes are expected. The name of the effect is derived from the location where the phenomenon was first noted, the Hawthorne plant of the Western Electric Company, in Chicago. In 1927, a series of changes—adjustments in light levels, more frequent or longer rest breaks—were made to the work environment at this plant in an attempt to determine which change or changes would improve worker productivity the most. The plant workers were told in advance what the change was, when it would occur, and what the researchers expected the outcome to be. Not surprisingly, the expected outcomes did materialize (Gillespie 1991).

Mentally ill patients taking prescription drugs undergo orientation similar to that received by the Hawthorne plant workers. First, they are told that their illness is caused by a chemical imbalance in the brain. Then they are told that they will be given a medication that will put the chemicals in proper balance, and that their behavior will subsequently change. What really prompts the behavioral change may be the salting of the mind with expectations that have no lasting effect, as evidenced by the increase in the number of mentally ill people now being sent to prison. If this is the case, then there is no reason to believe that criminal behavior is caused by a chemical imbalance or that altering the chemical balance will prevent it. Alternatively, it may be that many mentally ill individuals lack the self-discipline required to continue taking their medication when they are not under the constant supervision provided in an institutional setting. In this case, the increase in the number of mentally ill persons in prisons might be the result of eliminating mental health institutional space, and not because the chemical treatment was ineffective.

As early as 1975, psychiatrists from several different countries (the Germans Otto Benkert, Hanns Hippius, Peter Mueller, Hans-Joachim Hasse, and Baerbel Armbruster; the Swiss Raymond Bettegay, Annemarie Gehring, Walter Poeldinger, and Hiri Modestin; Norwegian Rolf Hessoe; and the Englishman Peter Lehmann) began publishing warnings about the unintended depressive effects of some psychiatric medications, which resulted in an increased number of suicides. Some psychiatrists go so far as to say that psychiatric drugs may do more harm than good. Peter R. Breggin, International Director of the Center for the Study of Psychiatry and Psychology in Baltimore, Maryland, and David Cohen, a professor of social work and researcher in the field of psychiatric medications, are the coauthors of the book *How Your Drug May Be Your Problem: How and Why to Stop Taking Psychiatric Medications.* Breggin and Cohen say that psychiatric drugs can cause serious side effects, and can even ruin a patient's health and life (Breggin and Cohen 1999).

In March 2004, the Federal Drug Administration (FDA) in the United States took heed of these warnings and allegations, and issued a public health advisory suggesting that doctors, patients, patients' families, and other caregivers be watchful for signs of increased depression or suicidal thoughts at the onset of psychotropic drug therapy, and whenever a patient's dose is changed. In addition, the FDA asked pharmaceutical manufacturers to add warnings to the labels of ten different antidepressant medications: Prozac, Paxil, Zoloft, Effexor, Celexa, Remeron, Lexapro, Luvox, Serzone, and Wellbutrin. (A similar warning was issued by health officials in Great Britain in 2003.) In October 2004, the FDA issued a directive requiring all drug manufacturers to attach a "black box" warning label—the FDA's strongest warning label—to all antidepressants, informing the user that there is a link between antidepressants and increased suicidal thoughts and behavior among children and teens who take them (CNN, March 22, 2004).

Chapter 6

PSYCHOLOGICAL DETERMINISM

The basic premise of the psychological determinism theory is that abnormal behavior, including criminal behavior, is learned—either from traumatic events that occurred in early childhood or from events and experiences that result in the development of false perceptions and irrational beliefs about the surrounding world. Abnormal behavior is generally divided into three categories: psychotic disorders, neurotic disorders, and personality disorders (Kalat 2005).

Psychotic Disorders

In the simplest terms, psychotic disorders are characterized by one's inability to distinguish right from wrong, or to differentiate fantasy from reality. Hallucinations—either auditory, visual, or both—are common indicators of psychotic behavior. If an individual commits a crime and is found to have been psychotic at the time the crime was committed, he or she will likely be found not responsible due to a mental disease or defect, or not guilty by reason of insanity.

In lieu of being punished, criminal offenders diagnosed as psychotic are normally placed in a hospital for the mentally ill. They remain hospitalized until a court examines reports from the individual's attending psychiatrist and determines that the mental illness is in remission, and that the person will no longer constitute a threat to others if released from the hospital. Some states, such as Oregon, have established an independent board to review psychiatrists' recommendations, and to make the decision either to release the individual from hospital confinement, or to order him or her to continue inpatient treatment (MacKay 1995).

Neurotic Disorders

Neurotic disorders characteristically involve extreme anxiety triggered by an unfounded fear or threat, physical complaints for which there is no known cause, or obsessive thoughts and compulsive acts that drastically interfere with normal life. People with compulsive disorders, for example, may spend hours washing their hands after going to the bathroom in response to obsessive and irrational thoughts about bacterial disease (Martin 1971).

Personality Disorders

The American Psychiatric Association's generic definition of a personality disorder is "an enduring pattern of
inner experience and behavior that deviates markedly from
the expectation of the individual's culture, is pervasive and
inflexible, has an onset in adolescence or early adulthood,
is stable over time and leads to distress or impairment."
There are ten distinct personality disorders:

Antisocial Personality Disorder
Avoidant Personality Disorder
Borderline Personality Disorder
Dependent Personality Disorder
Histrionic Personality Disorder
Narcissistic Personality Disorder
Obsessive-Compulsive Personality Disorder
Paranoid Personality Disorder
Schizoid Personality Disorder
Schizotype Personality Disorder
(American Psychiatric Association 2000)

Most criminals are classified as having an antisocial personality disorder, and display traits that are sometimes
called psychopathic or sociopathic. A person with an antisocial personality disorder is typically manipulative, impul-

sive, and deceitful, and possesses no sense of remorse. He or she shows little or no regard for laws, rules, or the rights of others; and is often unable or unwilling to sustain personal relationships with friends, family, employers, or coworkers, unless it is profitable for them to do so (Malloy 1988).

The general public and the media often use the term psychotic and psychopathic interchangeably because it is hard for any rational person to understand how a human being could knowingly commit a criminal act—particularly a brutal act of violence against another person—unless the offender is psychotic and does not understand what he or she is doing. Psychopaths are not psychotic. Psychopaths know what they are doing and they know if what they are doing is right or wrong—they simply don't care

Psychological Treatment Modalities

Those who believe that criminal behavior is psychologically determined usually advocate some form of psychotherapy often supplemented with psychotropic medications. There are multiple types of psychotherapy, but the approaches most commonly used are psychoanalysis-psychodynamic therapy, interpersonal therapy, and cognitive-behavioral therapy (George 1990).

Psychoanalysis-Psychodynamic Therapy

The basic premise of psychoanalysis-psychodynamic therapy is that abnormal behavior is the product of conflict between an individual's defense mechanisms and unwanted memories of bad childhood experiences hidden in an individual's subconscious mind. Based on theories first proposed by Sigmund Freud in the late nineteenth century, the remedy or treatment for abnormal behavior caused by these conflicts is to release these hidden feelings from the subconscious through conversation, a process sometimes called "talk therapy." Through the use of a dialogue with a patient, a psychotherapist attempts to help the patient understand the origin of his or her inner conflict, and the feelings generated by this conflict. The theory is that once the individual understands these feelings, the conflict will subside and the abnormal behavior it is causing becomes more susceptible to change (Corey 1991).

Interpersonal Therapy

Interpersonal therapy is similar to psychoanalytic-psychodynamic therapy in that it also involves an ongoing conversation between a therapist and a patient. In this case, however, the focus of the conversation is on current events in the patient's life, such as the death of a loved one, unwanted or unexpected employment status changes, geographical relocation, or marital or family conflict that may be the underlying causes of the person's behavioral problems (Ivey et al. 2002).

Cognitive-Behavioral Therapy

Cognitive-behavioral therapy is based on the idea that behavior is the product of an individual's conscious beliefs and perceptions, and not of unconscious conflicts caused by traumatic early life experiences. How a person feels and behaves is the result of how a person thinks, and not the consequence of external events or the actions of other people. Abnormal behavior occurs as a result of "thinking errors," which have their origins in false perceptions and irrational beliefs. It is the individual's mistaken beliefs or perception of life's events, as opposed to the events themselves that generate erroneous thinking; and erroneous thinking results in behavior that is unacceptable, destructive, and harmful to the person, others or both (Anderson 1995).

Unlike psychodynamic and interpersonal therapies, which are fluid, flexible, and open-ended, cognitive-behavioral therapy, although collaborative, is highly structured and more goal-directed, with the patient and therapist performing interdependent but different roles. The goal of cognitive therapy is to identify and eliminate the errors in a person's thought processes and replace them with those that produce more desirable feelings and behavior. The role of the therapist is to listen, teach and encourage. The role of the patient is to speak, learn, and implement what is learned. The duration of cognitive-behavioral therapy is typically much shorter than that of psychoanalytical therapy. It lasts only weeks, or perhaps months in more complex cases, as opposed to the many years a course of psychoanalytical therapy might last. The duration of cognitive-behavioral therapy is shorter partly because the methods it uses are more structured than those used in psychoanalytical therapy.

In the mid 1990s, Samuel Yochelson and Stanton Samenow coauthored *The Criminal Personality, Volume I: A Profile for Change* (1994) and *Criminal Personality, Volume II: The Change Process* (1995). These two publications are the culmination of a fourteen-year study conducted by the authors as part of the Program for the Investigation of Criminal Behavior at St. Elizabeth's Hospital, a division of the National Institute of Mental Health in Washington DC.

Initially, Yochelson—who started the study—was seeking to discover what causes criminal behavior and to determine how the behavior could be changed using traditional psychotherapeutic techniques. After four years, he concluded that he had made no progress toward finding a cause for criminal behavior. He also concluded that traditional psychotherapeutic methods are not only ineffective for dealing with criminal behavior, but are also based on an incorrect premise—that criminal behavior, like all behavior, is learned through life experiences. After reviewing the results from the first fours years of the study, Yochelson and Samenow came to the conclusion that criminal behavior is a rational choice made on the basis of irrational thinking ("thinking errors") and that attributing the origins of criminal behavior to unfortunate life experiences—whether psychological or social—allows criminals to justify their behavior and blame others for who they are and what they do (Yochelson & Samenow, 1994).

Abandoning the goal of finding a cause for criminal behavior, Yochelson and Samenow started a new study based on the premise that criminal behavior is the combined result of specific personality traits and a particular thinking process. According to the two researchers, criminals are manipulative, restless, dissatisfied, irritable, selfish, demanding, coercive, scheming, and driven by an insatiable need for excitement and self-satisfaction, no matter what the cost. Criminals believe that rules and laws are for others. Criminals view people (family and friends included) as objects whose needs, wants, and expectations are impositions to be ignored unless they serve the criminal's interest. For criminals to change, concluded Yochelson and Samenow, they must be shown the errors in their thinking, and must be taught new ways of thinking. However, before criminals can be taught how to change, they must reach the conclusion that change will be beneficial, which will most likely not happen until they hit rock bottom. Out of the 255 participants that started the program, only 30 followed it to completion, and only 9 demonstrated signs of genuine change as Yochelson and Samenow chose to measure it. Yochelson's and Samenow's own best estimate is that the cognitive-behavioral approach will benefit no more than 20 percent of the criminal population, which is no better than the recidivism rate for criminals who spend an unspecified term in prison, unexposed to any form of treatment (Samenow 2002; Yochelson and Samenow 1995).

The validity of the idea that traumatic life experiences are the root causes of criminal behavior is highly suspect for one simple reason: most people who suffer traumatic life experiences do not become criminals. Trauma, like stress, is relative. What is traumatic or stressful for one person may not be traumatic or stressful for another. Each person responds to trauma and stress in a different way. Some people become emotionally upset and exhibit behavioral problems when they are required to perform multiple tasks, or when they feel intense pressure to complete a task by a specific time. For others, idleness is toxic. This second group is less likely to become emotionally upset or exhibit behavioral problems when they have multiple balls in the air or are striving to complete a task in the face of what others might perceive as overwhelming obstacles. But even if traumatic life experiences were the root cause for criminal behavior, psychotherapy would not prevent criminal behavior.

In America, individual rights usually take precedence over government authority. Government agencies are prohibited from intervening in private family matters unless a law is broken. There are no restrictions on who can conceive children, and there are no uniform standards for parenting that must be satisfied. As will be discussed in more detail later, socioeconomic conditions in the United States vary widely, and under these circumstances there is no way to eliminate traumatic life experiences or to prevent the formation of irrational beliefs or false perceptions. The best result psychotherapy can provide—whether it be after a course of psychoanalysis, interpersonal therapy, or cognitive-behavioral therapy—is a means to eliminate criminal behavior after a criminal act has been committed; and the odds of achieving even this outcome are not favorable.

Psychotherapy cannot prevent criminal behavior; it can only assist those who have already shown themselves to be criminals. And even in this regard, the results to date are less than encouraging.

Chapter 7

SOCIOLOGICAL DETERMINISM

The basic premise of sociological determinism is that criminal behavior is caused by substandard living conditions and certain environmental circumstances: poverty, unemployment, hunger, poor health care, substandard housing, and illiteracy (Alexander et al. 1999; Alexander and Smith 2005). A review of the data that describe how wealth, jobs, housing, food, health care, and education are currently distributed in the United States clearly indicates there is great disparity.

Poverty

Poverty levels in America are calculated by both the Census Bureau and the Department of Health and Human Services. Because these two government agencies make their calculations for different reasons, they use different formulas. The Census Bureau uses its calculations to estimate the number Americans living in poverty. The Health and Human Services department uses its calculations to determine eligibility for federal assistance programs. This discussion will focus on the results produced by the Census Bureau. The formula used by the Census

Bureau is based on three criteria: income before taxes, family size, and family composition. Using these criteria, the Census Bureau established the following:

- There were 37.0 million people below the poverty line in 2005, which was 1.7 million more than in 2001.

- Just over twelve million (12.1 million) of the total number living below the poverty line in 2005 were children under the age of eighteen, compared to 11.7 million in 2001.

- The number of people between the ages of eighteen and sixty-four living below the poverty line increased from 17.8 million in 2001 to 20.5 million in 2005.

- The number of elderly (those people over the age of sixty-four) below the poverty line increased from 3.4 million in 2001 to 3.6 million in 2005.

Table 6: Census Bureau Poverty Thresholds for 2005

Size of Family Unit	Related children under 18 years								
	None	One	Two	Three	Four	Five	Six	Seven	Eight or more
One person 65< >65	10,160 9,367								
Two people Householder 65< Householder >65	13,078 11,805	13,461 13,410							
Three people	15,557	15,277	15,720						
Four people	20,144	20,474	19,806	19,874					
Five people	24,293	24,646	23,891	23,307	22,951				
Six people	27,941	28,052	27,474	26,920	26,096	25,608			
Seven people	32,150	32,350	31,658	31,176	30,277	29,229	28,079		
Eight people	35,957	36,274	35,621	35,049	34,237	33,207	32,135	31,862	
Nine people or more	43,254	43,463	42,885	42,400	41,603	40,507	39,515	39,270	37,757

Unemployment

In America, for the most part, one's income is dependent on having a job. Unfortunately, not all Americans have jobs. The U.S. Department of Labor defines an unemployed worker as "any person sixteen years or older who is not working, is available for work, and has made specific efforts to find work during the previous four weeks." This definition is further refined into four different categories of unemployment: frictional, structural, cyclical, and seasonal.

- Frictional unemployment accounts for those individuals who are between jobs, but are expected to start a new job soon.

- Structural unemployment accounts for those individuals who are unemployed because labor market needs have changed and certain types of jobs are no longer required.

- Cyclical unemployment accounts for those individuals who are unemployed because demand for a product or service has diminished.

- Seasonal unemployment accounts for those individuals who are unemployed because their work is related to or controlled by conditions prevalent only at a particular time of year.

To calculate the unemployment rate, the Department of Labor divides the total number of unemployed workers by the number of people in the civilian labor force. The civilian labor force is the combined total number of employed and unemployed workers. Using this formula, the average unemployment rate in the United States for the ten-year period from 1994 through 2003 was 5.1 percent, which translates to over fourteen million people at any given time (Bureau of Labor Statistics 2004).

Table 7: Unemployment Rates in the United States

	Jan	Feb	Mar	Apr	May	June	July	Aug	Sept	Oct	Nov	Dec	Yr
1994–2003													
1994	6.6	6.5	6.5	6.4	6.1	6.1	6.1	6.0	5.9	5.8	5.6	5.5	6.1
1995	5.6	5.4	5.4	5.8	5.6	5.6	5.7	5.6	5.6	5.5	5.6	5.6	5.6
1996	5.6	5.5	5.5	5.6	5.6	5.3	5.5	5.1	5.2	5.2	5.4	5.4	5.4
1997	5.3	5.2	5.5	5.1	4.9	5.0	4.8	4.9	4.7	4.7	4.6	4.7	4.9
1998	4.6	4.6	4.7	4.3	4.4	4.5	4.5	4.5	4.6	4.5	4.4	4.4	4.5
1999	4.3	4.4	4.2	4.3	4.2	4.3	4.3	4.2	4.2	4.1	4.1	4.0	4.2
2000	4.0	4.1	4.0	3.8	4.0	4.0	4.0	4.1	4.0	3.9	3.9	3.9	4.0
2001	4.2	4.2	4.3	4.4	4.3	4.5	4.6	4.9	5.0	5.4	5.6	5.7	4.8
2002	5.6	5.7	5.7	5.9	5.8	5.8	5.8	5.7	5.7	5.7	5.9	6.0	5.8
2003	5.8	5.9	5.8	6.0	6.1	6.3	6.2	6.1	6.1	6.0	5.9	5.7	6.0

Major concern is currently being expressed about the significant decline in the number of jobs available to American workers as a result of foreign outsourcing. From January 2001 to January 2004, an estimated three million jobs were eliminated in the United States. Most of the jobs lost have been in manufacturing, and many of these jobs were transferred to foreign countries where labor is cheaper. The loss of jobs to other countries is not a new issue. Robert Reich, Secretary of Labor during President Clinton's first term, discusses this phenomenon in depth in his book *The Work of Nations*, published in 1991. The difference between then and now is that today, many jobs are also being lost in the information technology and telecommunications sectors. In late 2003, Forrester Research, a national consulting firm, surveyed 145 companies in the United States and concluded that "over the next fifteen years, 3.3 million service-industry jobs will move offshore to countries like India, Russia, China, and the Philippines" (McCarthy et al. 2004).

In response to the expressions of concern about jobs being lost to overseas workers, Allen Greenspan, former Chairman of the Federal Reserve Bank, announced that the steady movement of U.S. jobs offshore is good for the economy in the long run, but that American workers need to be better educated to be qualified for whatever higher-skilled jobs materialize to replace the jobs that have been lost (Gongloff 2004). As will be discussed later, at a time when more people need higher education, access to it is becoming increasingly unobtainable by a growing number of America's youth. Nearly 30 percent of high-school-age-kids drop out of school before they receive a diploma, and fewer than 50 percent of those who do graduate from high school and are academically qualified to enroll in college are unable to do so because it is too costly. Therefore, Greenspan's advice about how to repair the economy and prepare for a changing labor market may be as impractical as the advice given to Mrs. Winchester for ridding her house of ghosts.

Substandard Housing

There are two different groups that must be included in any discussion regarding housing. The first group includes those who have some form of housing that is either owned or rented. The second group includes the homeless—those who have no housing at all.

Owner-Occupied or Rented Housing

The U.S. Census Bureau reports that in 2001, 68 percent of all housing was owner-occupied and 32 percent was rented. The median value of owner-occupied dwellings was $123,887, while the median monthly housing cost (including rent, utilities, and garbage collection) for a renter totaled $633, which was 29 percent of the average renter's income. The National Low Income Housing Coalition (NLIHC) says that the Census Bureau's data grossly underestimate the extent of the problem because the Census Bureau formula does not account for the affordability of housing. The NLIHC measures affordable housing by the number of households with housing problems of substandard living conditions, overcrowding, and a housing cost in excess of 30 percent of the household income. Using its criteria, the NLIHC reports that 36,900,000, or 31 percent, of all households in the United States had housing problems in 2001. In the final analysis, the difference between the estimate developed by the Census Bureau and the estimate developed by the NLIHC is of no practical value, but one thing remains certain:

securing and maintaining housing is a major problem for the 34.6 million people whose income is at or below the poverty line.

The Homeless

In addition to those individuals who are can afford no better than substandard housing, there are those who can afford no housing at all. Quantifying how many people are homeless is difficult because being homeless is typically a temporary circumstance not a static condition, and because the homeless who are counted are only those who can be easily found in shelters, soup kitchens, and similar environments that are operated by government or private nonprofit agencies. Homeless people who live in rural areas, suburbs, or places that are not easily accessible, such as under bridges or viaducts, are often not included in official estimates of the homeless. As a result, estimates of how many people are homeless in the United States range from 840,000 to 1.35 million on any given day (U.S. Department of Housing and Urban Development 2001).

Hunger

No one is surprised to learn that people go hungry in undeveloped countries. But it would probably come as a shock to most Americans to learn that there are large numbers of people in the United States who suffer from hunger. The U.S. Department of Agriculture refers to these people as being "food insecure," which in their parlance means someone who does not have "access at all times to enough food to live an active, healthy life" (U.S. Department of Agriculture 2004).

The U.S. Census Bureau periodically conducts a survey for the U.S. Department of Agriculture to assess the scope of the hunger problem in the United States. The survey sample consists of about 50,000 households. Each household surveyed is asked eighteen questions designed to determine how much the house hold spends on food, whether it used various public food-assistance programs and whether it was consistently able to get enough food to meet the needs of all household members. Households surveyed are then classified as food-secure, food-insecure without hunger, or food-insecure with hunger. The results of the survey conducted in December 2001 reveal the following:

- 11.5 million households (10.7 percent of all U.S. households) had been food-insecure at some point during the year.

- 3.5 million households (3.3 percent of all U.S. households) were food-insecure with hunger, which means that one or more members of the household had been hungry at least occasionally during the year because they couldn't afford enough food.

- 211,000 of the 3.5 million food-insecure house-holds included children.

Poor Health Care

Access to health care in the United States is not considered a basic right of every citizen. Health care is big business in the United States, and patients must pay for the service. Most Americans rely on health insurance, for which they pay a monthly premium, to help defray the cost. In some instances, a person's employer pays the premium in whole or in part. Sixty-two percent of all full-time and part-time employees participate in a group health plan provided by their employers. Nevertheless, according to Census Bureau data, 46.6 million Americans under the age of sixty-five were uninsured at some point during 2005. More than 8 percent (8.3 percent) of those uninsured were children under the age of eighteen. In addition to the cost of the premium, four-fifths of worker policies now require the insured to pay a deductible before their insurance pays benefits. The average deductible is $384 for single coverage and $785 for family coverage, excluding a separate $202 deductible for inpatient care (US Bureau of Census 2005).

Illiteracy

Higher Education is touted as the great equalizer in American society. It is promoted as the one thing that can give every citizen in our nation—regardless of race, gender, income, or location—the same opportunity to succeed. Although this belief may very well be true, unfortunately not all students have equal access to higher education.

One reason many students do not have equal access to higher education is that they are unable to meet the academic entrance requirements for enrollment in four-year colleges and universities. According to the National Center for Education Statistics, the average drop-out rate (the percentage of students who quit school without earning a diploma) from public schools in 2001 was 28.9 percent for students aged fifteen and sixteen, 34.1 percent for seventeen-year-old students, and 26.9 percent for eighteen-year-old students. Overall, the average drop-out rate that year for students between the ages of fifteen and eighteen was 29.96 percent—which, incidentally, is comparable to the recidivism rate for most prisons. In 2001, the United States Census Bureau reported that 20,219,890 individuals out of the country's entire population of 281,421,906 were between the ages of fifteen and nineteen, which suggests that approximately six million young people living in the United States at that time did not have access to higher education because they did not finish high school.

A second reason many students are denied equal access to higher education is that they lack the financial resources required to pay the cost of tuition, fees, books, lodging, and food. According to the College Board—perhaps best known for administering the Scholastic Aptitude Test (SAT), which is used by most colleges and universities to help them to decide whether or not to admit a student applicant—the average total cost for tuition, fees, lodging, and food for the academic school year 2005–2006 was $12,127 at a four-year public institution, and $29,026 at a four-year private institution. Unfortunately again, many academically qualified high school graduates cannot afford to go to college. In 2003, the House Committee on Education and the Workforce for the 108th Congress of the United States found that 48 percent of all academically qualified high school graduates could not afford to attend a four-year college or university, and that 22 percent of them could not afford to attend a college of any kind. The committee estimated that if this rate were to continue, by the end of the decade two million college-qualified students would be completely denied the opportunity for a postsecondary education. The substance of the committee's finding was confirmed in 2004 by the National

Center for Public Policy and Higher Education—an independent, nonprofit, nonpartisan organization unaffiliated with any government agency, political party, college, or university that conducts policy research on public policy issues affecting education and training beyond the high-school level. This organization has concluded that even though financial aid has increased, the rising cost of attending college has "outpaced the growth in family income." College, for most Americans, is less affordable today than it was a decade ago.

Although there is general agreement about what social factors promote criminal behavior (poverty, unemployment, substandard housing, hunger, poor health care, and illiteracy) there are a number of different theories about how these social factors interact to promote criminal behavior. The discussion that follows will feature seven of the more prominent theories.

Cultural Deviance or Subculture Theory

Among the early scholarly works to advance the culture deviance/subculture theory were: Wolfgang and Ferracuti 1967; Cloward and Ohlin 1960; Cohen 1955; and Miller 1958. According to this theory, individuals who exhibit criminal behavior are typically reared in environments characterized by slum conditions: low income, racial and ethnic segregation, poor health care, high divorce rates, and elevated school drop-out rates. Such conditions breed a subculture with a deviant value system that is in conflict with the values of the law-abiding population.

Strain Theory

The desire for money is the driving force behind strain theory. Strain theory proponents argue that when low-income individuals are unable to improve their economic status, they are forced to resort to criminal behavior (Agnew 2002).

Structural Theory

Structural theory is a variation of strain theory. Its essence is that criminal behavior stems from the creation of false expectations. According to structural theory, children in America are raised to believe that anyone can become president or a millionaire; but the reality is that the structure of society permits only a select few to achieve such goals. The frustration generated when confronted with the reality that equal opportunity is a myth results in criminal behavior (Merton 1996).

Social Control Theory

Social control theory assumes that all human beings are antisocial by nature. Non-criminals are those individuals who learn to control their antisocial instincts through associations with and instruction from others in society who have acquired a belief in and respect for the law—others such as parents, teachers, friends, clergy, and coaches. Individuals who grow up without the benefit of these positive influences are more likely to engage in criminal activity, regardless of their socio-economic background, education, or family history (Hirschi 1969).

Social Disorganization Theory

The concept of social disorganization theory was first advanced by French sociologist Emile Durkheim in the late 1890s. Durkheim postulated that societies develop through a two-stage process. In the first phase (the mechanical phase) people are more homogenous. They perform basically the same work, live by a common set of rules, and generally think and behave alike. In the second phase (the organic phase) life is more complex and people are more diverse. There is less of a sense of community, and people no longer share a cultural bond. Deviant behavior, including criminal behavior, occurs when the rules, norms, and behavioral expectations by which people live are undefined, confused, or unclear. Social control, which is a by-product of shared goals and norms, ceases to exist. Durkheim referred to this condition as *anomie* (Alexander and Smith 2005).

In the 1920s, a group of faculty members (George H. Mead, Ellsworth Faris, Herbert Blumer, and Robert Park) at the University of Chicago's department of sociology refined Durkheim's concept into what became known as the Chicago school of empirical sociology. The approach used by the Chicago school was to remove the study of human beings from the classroom and conduct it in the communities where people lived and worked. The principal thesis of the Chicago school's philosophy was that human beings are innately social creatures, and as such their behavior was the product of their social environment. Through direct observation, Chicago-school investigators concluded that as a result of urbanization, industrialization, and mass migration into inner cities, the basic institutions of society—family, friendships, and other social groups—fragmented, creating separate groups and communities with conflicting norms and value systems. Absent a common value system, multiple diverse groups with conflicting values formed, fostering an array of social problems including criminal activity (Blumer 1984).

Labeling Theory

According to labeling theory, criminal behavior is neither right nor wrong. "Criminal behavior" is a label attached to any behavior that deviates from the norm as defined by people with power—parents, teachers, judges, and lawmakers—in an attempt to shame the individual into conformity. Two things happen when an individual's behavior is labeled. First, the individual is stigmatized and shunned by non-deviant members of society. Second, the individual adopts the labeled behavior as a lifestyle. All human beings need to feel accepted. Unable to find acceptance in mainstream society, the "criminal" finds it through association with others similarly labeled. After being labeled a criminal, the individual takes on the role and lifestyle he or she has been assigned and abandons any further attempt at conforming to social norms. Frank Tannenbaum (*Crime and the Community*, 1938), Edwin Lemert (*Social Pathology: A Systematic Approach to the Theory of Sociopathic Behavior*, 1951), and Howard Becker (*Outsiders: Studies in the Sociology of Deviance*, 1963) are among the more notable early proponents of labeling theory. Tannenbaum, referring to labeling as the "dramatization of evil," says that labeling evokes the very behavior it finds offensive. In the end, the individuals become what they have previously merely been accused of being. Lemert characterizes the process of labeling as the "societal reaction approach," which manifests itself in two different forms of deviance: primary deviance and secondary deviance. Primary deviance occurs when an individual behaves—for sociological, psychological, or biological reasons that are beyond his or her control—in a way that is considered deviant. Secondary deviance forms as a defensive reaction in response to society's reaction to the primary deviance. Becker believes that most people harbor deviant thoughts. Most of them control their thoughts and do not act out their deviance, while others are unable or unwilling to control their thoughts and do act them out. According to Becker, labeling is a three-step process. The initial and most crucial step occurs the moment an individual is first caught and assigned the label of criminal by a higher authority. The second step occurs when the individual surrenders to the consensus, accepts the label assigned by others, and begins to view himself as a criminal. The third step occurs when the individual fully adopts the role of a criminal and makes it a lifestyle.

Reintegrative Shaming Theory (Restorative Justice)

The concept of reintegrative shaming, also referred to as restorative justice, was first proposed in the late 1980s by

John Braithwaite, a professor in the law program in the Research School of Social Sciences at Australian National University and author of *Crime, Shame, and Reintegration.* A form of labeling theory, reintegrative shame theory argues that labeling can serve as a catalyst for positive change if the focus is placed on condemning the offensive behavior rather than on condemning the offender. The objectives of the traditional criminal justice system, say reintegrative shame theorists, are to determine what law was broken, to identify who broke the law, and to punish law violators. The process of reintegrative shame is built on the premise that if the focus is on restoration, as opposed to retribution, shame can invoke feelings of remorse; allow a person to accept responsibility for bad behavior, and lead them to refrain from blaming others. Theoretically, restorative shame will give satisfaction to the victims of crime, because the objective is to reintegrate the criminal into the main stream of society, and not to ostracize the person (Braithwaite 1989).

Ron Classen, director of the Center for Peacemaking and Conflict Studies at Fresno Pacific University, developed the following list of principles that are fundamental to the practice of restorative justice (Classen 1995). These principles are unedited as required by the author for reprinting.

- Crime is primarily an offense against human relationships, and secondarily a violation of law (since laws are written to protect safety and fairness in human relationships). Restorative Justice recognizes that crime (violations of persons and relationships) is wrong and should not occur; and also recognizes that after it does occur there are dangers and opportunities. The danger is that the community, victim(s), and/or offender emerge from the response further alienated, more damaged, disrespected, disempowered, feeling less cooperative with society. The opportunity is that injustice is recognized, the equity is restored (restitution and grace), and the future is clarified so that participants are safer, more respectful, and more empowered and cooperative with each other and society.

- Restorative Justice is a process to "make things as right as possible," which includes: attending to needs created by the offense such as safety and repair of injuries to relationships and physical damage resulting from the offense; and attending to needs related to the cause of the offense (addictions, lack of social or employment skills or resources, lack of moral or ethical base).

- The primary victim(s) of a crime is/are the one(s) most impacted by the offense. The secondary victims are others impacted by the crime and might include family members, friends, witnesses, criminal justice officials, and community.

- As soon as immediate victim, community, and offender safety concerns are satisfied, Restorative Justice views the situation as a teachable moment for the offender; an opportunity to encourage the offender to learn new ways of acting and being in the community.

- Restorative Justice prefers responding to the crime at the earliest point possible and with the maximum amount of voluntary cooperation and minimum coercion, since healing in relationships and new learning are voluntary and cooperative.

- Restorative Justice prefers that most crimes are handled using a cooperative structure including those impacted by the offense as a community to provide support and accountability. This might include primary and secondary victims and family (or substitutes if they choose not to participate), the offender and family, community representatives, government representatives, faith community representatives, and school representatives.

- Restorative Justice recognizes that not all offenders will choose to be cooperative. Therefore, there is a need for outside authority to make decisions for the offender who is not cooperative. The actions of the authorities and the consequences imposed should be tested by whether they are reasonable, restorative, and respectful for victim(s), offender, and community.

- Restorative Justice prefers that offenders who pose significant safety risks and are not yet cooperative be placed in settings where the emphasis is on safety, values, ethics, responsibility, accountability, and civility. They should be exposed to the impact of their crime(s) on victims, invited to learn empathy, and offered learning opportunities to become better equipped with skills to be productive members of society. They should continually be invited (not coerced) to become cooperative with the community, and be given the opportunity to demonstrate this in appropriate settings as soon as possible.

- Restorative Justice requires follow-up and accountability structures utilizing the natural community as much as possible, since keeping agreements is the key to building a trusting community.

- Restorative Justice recognizes and encourages the role of community institutions, including the religious/faith community in teaching and establishing the moral and ethical standards which build up the community.

To prevent criminal behavior and eliminate the need for after-the-fact remedial intervention, sociological theory argues that society must implement policies that will redistribute wealth, eliminate racism and discrimination, provide housing, jobs and health care for everyone, and guarantee equal access to education. If everyone were to have a job, adequate income, proper housing, food, health care, and an education, there would be no need to commit crimes in order to exist. To fully test the validity of the sociological school of thought, and to ensure total equality among all Americans, would require the complete reconstruction of the United States' economic and social systems, which is highly unlikely to happen.

Until a socio-economic paradigm shift occurs and the premise of this theory can be tested, the validity of sociological thinking appears vulnerable in at least two respects. First, even if criminal behavior is caused by socioeconomic factors, sociological theory fails to explain why all people who are products of poor socioeconomic circumstances do not become criminals. Second, sociological theory fails to account for white-collar crime, which is, according to Edwin Sutherland—the person credited with having coined the term—"a crime committed by a person of respectability and high social status in the course of his occupation"(Sutherland, 1949).

Chapter 8

REHABILITATION

The rehabilitation approach to crime prevention is an adaptation of the medical model. Introduced in the 1950s, the rehabilitation model promised, like all of its predecessors, to halt the rising crime rate, or at least reduce the possibility that former inmates would continue to violate the law when released from prison. The philosophy of the rehabilitation approach is based on the premise that the criminal is in some way lacking the necessary coping skills or abilities to succeed in life without committing crime. The belief is that criminal behavior can be reduced by eliminating the factor or factors that limit an individual's ability to succeed without resorting to criminal activity.

The first step in the rehabilitation process is a comprehensive "need assessment." After a criminal is convicted, he or she undergoes a complete medical/dental examination and is subjected to a battery of psychological, academic, and vocational aptitude tests. In addition, a complete social history—which includes family history, work history, education history, and prior criminal history—is collected and documented. The need assessment can be completed prior to sentencing, and can be used by the court to decide whether to sentence a criminal to a prison term or to place the individual on probation. Alternatively, the need assessment can be completed after the person is sentenced and incarcerated. The results of the need assessment are used to design a customized treatment plan. An offender who is unable to read or write is enrolled in a remedial education program. An offender who does not have a high-school diploma is enrolled in a secondary education program. An offender who has no employment skills is enrolled in a vocational training program. If the individual is a sex offender, or if testing and social history indicate that the offender has a psychological problem or history of substance abuse, the offender will be enrolled in an appropriate treatment program (Van Voorhis Braswell, and Lester 2004).

Substance-Abuse Rehabilitation Programs

In the past two decades, heavy emphasis has been placed on the provision of substance-abuse treatment programs because the vast majority of all criminals reportedly have a substance-abuse problem, which suggests that there is a high correlation between substance abuse and criminal behavior. The Bureau of Justice Statistics estimates that 60 to 83 percent of all criminal offenders have used drugs at some time in their lives, which is twice the estimated rate of drug use by non-criminals (Mumola 1998).

Substance-abuse treatment programs use a variety of different approaches, including therapeutic communities, pharmacological maintenance, psychotherapy, and multi-modal interventions. Therapeutic communities will be discussed in chapter 12. Pharmacological maintenance involves the long-term use of substitute drugs that either replace the illicit drug or block the effects of the illicit drug. Methadone and buprenorphine, both narcotic analgesics, are used as substitutes for heroin, morphine, codeine, and other opiate derivatives. Antabuse, a disulfiram that blocks the oxidation of alcohol in the bloodstream, is used to discourage alcohol consumption. A person taking Antabuse who ingests even a small amount of alcohol will experience nausea, vomiting, profuse sweating, an intense headache, muscle pain, and blurred vision. Multi-modal interventions, as the name suggests, consist of some combination of inpatient and outpatient services, including medical care, vocational training, academic education, family therapy, pharmacological maintenance, group therapy, individual psychotherapy, and stress-management seminars (Office of National Drug Policy 2001).

Data collected by the Federal Bureau of Prisons—in follow-up surveys sent both to inmates who had successfully completed a substance-abuse treatment program and to those who had not—indicate that an inmate who completes a substance abuse program is 9 percent less likely to be rearrested within the first six months following release than an inmate that who does not complete such a program (Pelissier et al. 2001). Although some argue this data proves the value of substance abuse programs, the data is weak and unrevealing for two reasons. First, the survey data only provide a snapshot view of success or failure just six months after release, which is far too soon to draw any generalized conclusions. Second, the high rate of substance abuse by convicted criminals is only correlative evidence. Substance-abuse treatment might lower the probability that a convicted criminal will re-offend, but it does not establish a cause-and-effect relationship.

Sex Offender Rehabilitation Programs

Sex offenders provoke more debate over which approach is the best for dealing with criminals, than any other type of criminal, with the possible exception of murderers. From the classical school point of view, treatment for sex offenders is not only fruitless, but undeserved. To many in the general public, sex offenders are less than human, primarily because the victims of sex crimes are most often children or women. Even other criminals look down on sex offenders. In a prison environment, sex offenders are often ostracized, assaulted, or even killed by other inmates, just because they are sex offenders. Classical-school sanctions for sex offenses include castration, a life term in prison without the possibility of parole, and execution.

At the opposite end of the spectrum is the positivist-school point of view. Although there is a general consensus among positivist-school thinkers that punishment is not an effective sanction, there is disagreement over what causes a person to commit a sexual offense, and how best to treat the problem. The majority view seems to be that the cause of criminal sexual behavior is psychological in origin, and that the most appropriate sanction is some form of therapeutic intervention—psychotherapy, cognitive therapy, aversion therapy, or a combination of the three (Farkas and Stichman 2002; Winick and LaFond 2003; Rice and Harris 2003; Morse 2003). An alternative view of what causes an individual to become a sex offender—specifically, a rapist—has recently been proposed by Thornhill and Palmer (2000), and will be discussed in chapter 9.

Data collected by investigators examining recidivism rates for sex offenders suggest that treatment can lower the probability of an offender committing another sex offense upon release from confinement. The results of a meta-analysis completed in 1998 by Hanson and Bussiere indicate that 81 percent of the rapists and 87 percent of the child molesters involved in the sixty-one follow-up studies analyzed remained arrest-and/or conviction-free for a new sex offense after four to five years. In November 2003, the United States Bureau of Justice Statistics (BOJ) released the results of a recidivism study involving 9,691 sex offenders released in 1994 from prisons in Arizona, Maryland, North Carolina, California, Michigan, Ohio, Delaware, Minnesota, Oregon, Florida, New Jersey, Texas, Illinois, New York, and Virginia, that supported the findings of Hanson and Bussiere. The BOJ study found that within three years of release from prison, only 3.5 had been convicted of a new sex offense (Hanson and Bussiere 1998; Langan and Schmitt 2003).

Generalizations based on the data analyzed by these investigators should, however, be made with extreme caution, for two reasons. First, the methods used in the studies lacked uniformity. Second, the length of time used to measure success was short. It should also be noted that both Hanson/Bussiere and Langan/Schmitt reported that a significant number of sex offenders were rearrested or reconvicted of nonsexual crimes. Hanson and Bussiere found that in the studies they evaluated, nearly 37 percent of the child molesters and over 46 percent of the rapists went on to commit a nonsexual crime, while Langan and Schmitt reported that 24 percent were convicted of a new crime other than a sex offense, and 38.6 percent were returned to prison either because they committed a new crime or because they violated a condition of their parole.

Religious Rehabilitation Programs

Among those who advocate for rehabilitation are some who assert that religious intervention—in the form of Bible instruction and spiritual education and training—can effectively reduce criminal behavior.

CRIMINON, a program developed by L. Ron Hubbard, founder of the Church of Scientology; and Prison Fellowship, a religious ministry founded by Charles Colson, are two examples of religion-based rehabilitation programs. (Colson is a former aide to President Nixon, and an ex-convict who served a short prison term for his role in the burglary of the Watergate Hotel, which led to Nixon resigning in order to avoid impeachment.)

CRIMINON claims in its promotional literature that its program "eliminates any mystery about the sources of crime and demonstrates that crime has an exact cause— loss of self-respect—which can be addressed and resolved. Prison Fellowship's prognostications for success are less bold than those of CRIMINON (www.criminon.org and www.prisonfellowship.org).

Independent researchers from Lamar, Duke, and Morehead State Universities, after statistically analyzing data collected by the Prison Fellowship on 201 male inmates from four prisons who participated in Prison Fellowship programs while incarcerated and 201 inmates who did not participate in Prison Fellowship programs, found no overall difference in recidivism between the two groups. However, the researchers did conclude that inmates who participated in high-level Prison Fellowship-sponsored Bible studies while incarcerated were significantly less likely than nonparticipants—or than low-to medium-level participants—to be arrested during the first year following their release from prison. The researchers defined high-level participation as attendance at ten or more Bible studies during a one-year period (Johnson, Larson, and Pitts 1997).

Academic-Education and Vocational-Training Rehabilitation Programs

According to a report published by the Bureau of Justice Statistics in January 2003, an estimated 40 percent of state prison inmates, 27 percent of federal prison inmates, and 47 percent of local jail inmates for the years 1989 through

1997 did not have a high school diploma or GED (Harlow 2003).

The United States Department of Education conducts a periodic national survey to determine the literacy proficiencies of both the general population and the prison population. The results of the last survey, conducted in 2002, indicated that the average literacy proficiency of the prison population is substantially lower than that of the general population. Literacy is measured in three different categories: prose literacy, which involves the knowledge and skills to search, comprehend, and use information from continuous text; document literacy, which involves the knowledge and skills to search, comprehend, and use information from noncontinuous texts in various formats; and quantitative literacy, which involves the knowledge and skills to identify and perform computations, either alone or sequentially, using numbers embedded in printed material (Kutner, M., Greenberg, E., and Baer, J. 2005).

Table 8: Literacy Scores—Prison Population v. General Population

Population	Prose Scale	Document Scale	Quantitative Scale
Prison	246	240	236
General	275	271	283

Advocates for academic education and vocational training argue that providing criminals with academic education to enhance their literacy and ensuring that they are vocationally trained before release from prison will lower recidivism rates because the offender will be better prepared to secure and maintain gainful employment (MacCormick 1931; Harer 1995; Steurer, Smith, and Tracy 2001). Unfortunately, none of the research conducted to date into this question either supports or refutes this argument. Stefan LoBuglio, author of *Time to Reframe Politics and Practices in Correctional Education* says that for the past half-century, researchers have attempted—in literally thousands of studies—to find statistically significant and causal connections between treatment programming and recidivism, and have been unsuccessful. These failures are attributed by LoBuglio to poorly and inadequately designed education programs and flawed research methods. The vast majority of studies were retrospective in nature, says LoBuglio: researchers examined programs that had occurred in the past, and had no control over what data were collected. Because many studies were conducted by the agencies administering the programs, there was also an inherent bias in favor of positive findings. Most studies failed to consider the fact that educational programs may have attracted inmates who were more disposed to low recidivism rates. It is difficult for researchers to separate the effect of correctional education programs on recidivism rate reductions when more motivated and better prepared inmates self-select into programs (LoBuglio 2001; Wilson, Gallagher, and MacKenzie 2000).

Work Rehabilitation Programs

Most, if not all, prison systems in the United States require able-bodied inmates to work. Virtually all prisons and jails use inmate labor in the operation of the facility, both because it reduces operating costs and because it keeps prisoners constructively occupied. Work programs are often publicized and justified as being rehabilitative, ostensibly by teaching inmates good work habits, interpersonal skills, and new work skills, as well as by enhancing their self-esteem. Although hardly anyone would oppose requiring inmates to work, there is absolutely no empirical evidence to support the idea that requiring criminals to work while incarcerated reduces the probability of their re-offending upon release (Wilson, Gallager, and McKenzie 2000).

Oregon is the only state in America, and perhaps the only government entity in the world, that has a constitutional provision that requires inmates to work. In November 1994, Oregon voters approved the Prison Reform and Inmate Work Act, which was placed on the ballot by petition. The act amended the state constitution, mandating that "All inmates of state corrections institutions shall be actively engaged full-time in work or on-the-job training." Full-time is defined in the Oregon State Constitution as "the equivalent of at least forty hours per seven-day week." Education may be provided to inmates as part of work or on-the-job training, as long as each inmate is engaged at least half of the time in hands-on training or work activity. Inmates who are deemed by corrections officials to be physically or mentally disabled, too dangerous to society, or chemically dependent to the point they are unable to participate, may be exempt from work programs. Prisoners who are exempt because of chemical dependency must participate in appropriate drug or alcohol treatment, but prisoners who are deemed physically or mentally disabled or too dangerous are not required to participate in treatment programs. The Oregon State Constitution now declares that "Prison work programs shall be designed and carried out so as to achieve net cost savings in maintaining government operations or so as to achieve a net profit in private-sector activities," and further specifies that "Any compensation earned [by a prisoner] (and compensation is not mandatory) shall only be used for: (a) reimbursement of all or a portion of the inmate's rehabilitation, housing, health care, and living costs; (b) restitution or compensation to victims of the particular inmate's crime; (c) restitution or compensation to the victims of crime generally through a fund designed for this purpose; (d) financial support for immediate family of the inmate outside the corrections institution; and (e) payment of fines, court costs and applicable taxes." None of the money earned by the prison may be spent or saved at the discretion of the prisoner (Oregon State Constitution, Article 1, Section 41). By amending its state constitution to require that all inmates work forty hours per week, Oregon voters inadvertently have created a unique category of people—one whose members are guaranteed jobs—which is an assurance guaranteed to no law-abiding citizen anywhere else in the "free" world.

The most obvious limitation to any form of the rehabilitation approach is that it is potentially beneficial only to those criminals who are caught and sentenced; and even then it requires a strong commitment and high level of motivation on the part of the criminal. Obviously, rehabilitation will not prevent a person from becoming a criminal. It is not the rehabilitation program that changes the criminal's behavior; but the criminal himself or herself who is committed to change.

Chapter 9

SOCIOBIOLOGY AND EVOLUTIONARY PSYCHOLOGY

The basic premise of sociobiology and evolutionary psychology is the same, which is that the primary behavioral features of every human being, like the primary physical traits of every living organism, evolved over time by adapting to the surrounding environment; and that these traits are stored in the genes of every living organism. The major difference between evolutionary psychology and sociobiology is that the focus of the former is exclusively on understanding the behavior of humans only; whereas the latter explores the behavior of all living organisms. Adaptation in the evolutionary process is based on the biological principle that the physical characteristics found in contemporary animals—wings on birds, hands on humans, hoofs on horses, and gills on fish—are a direct result of the animal's ancestors having adapted to a problem that threatened their survival. Applied to human behavior, adaptation is the belief that phenol typical behavior (behavior that is readily observable in humans from the earliest stages of life) can also be traced to the ancestral need for behavioral change that would have enhanced the evolutionary prospects of the species.

Sociobiology

In 1975, Edward O. Wilson—a zoologist at Harvard University, winner of a two Pulitzer prizes, and world-renowned for his study of animal behavior, particularly that of ants—postulated that all animal behavior, including human behavior, is physiologically based in a genetic structure that has evolved over time through the same natural selection process as that through which physical characteristics are acquired, as described by Charles Darwin. "Sociobiology," a term Wilson borrowed from John P. Scott, a pioneer researcher in behavioral genetics, was selected by Wilson as the name of what he called "a new discipline." Sociobiology, Wilson says, is:

> ... a more explicitly hybrid discipline that incorporates knowledge from ethnology (the naturalistic study of whole patterns of behavior), ecology (the study of the relationships of organisms to their environment), and genetics in to order to derive general principles concerning the biological properties of entire societies. (*Sociobiology and Human Nature*, 1978)

Wilson acknowledges that some behavior is learned, to a degree, through environmental influences; but he believes that the basic features of human behavior—a tendency toward hierarchy, a deep personal concern about status and recognition, a tendency to place great value on self-esteem and individual integrity, a desire for personal privacy, a desire for deep sexual bonding and deep parental bonding, an aversion to incestuous behavior, and a tendency toward tribalism—are "hardwired" into the genes, just like the basic physical traits that have helped humans to survive and reproduce. Wilson believes that behaviors such as altruism, sexism, racism, selfishness, crime, aggression, and violence have all developed through the natural-selection process over millions of years.

Evolutionary Psychology

In 1992, psychologist Leda Cosmides and anthropologist John Tooby wrote an essay entitled "The Psychological Foundations of Culture," in which they argued that progress toward discovering the etiology of human behavior was hampered by a steadfast reliance on the standard belief that human beings are born without innate capacities, and also by a preoccupation with the desire to be kind and politically correct. Cosmides and Tooby—along with

Donald Symons, Margo Wilson, and Martin Daly—are credited with fostering the emergence of a new approach in the field of psychology: evolutionary psychology. Cosmides and Tooby deny that evolutionary psychology is their original idea, and attribute the underlying concept to William James, a late-nineteenth-century psychologist considered by many to be the founder of experimental psychology, and to George Williams, currently professor emeritus of ecology and evolution at the State University of New York at Stony Brook and author of *Adaptation and Natural Selection* (Crawford & Krebs 1998).

James took issue with the notion, which is still supported by many people today, that human beings, unlike other animals, have no instincts; that human beings have relinquished their instincts through the evolutionary process and have replaced them with the ability to reason; and that this is why human intelligence is more flexible than that of other animals. James, conversely, argued that human intelligence is more flexible than that of other animals because human beings have *more* instincts than other animals, not fewer. According to James, we do not recognize human behavior as instinctive because human instincts are so much more refined than animal instincts that we take many of them for granted.

George Williams's point of disagreement is with the idea that living organisms adapt to prevent the extinction of their own species. His position is that adaptations in individuals are the outcome of competition between individuals in the same group, rather than for the collective well-being of the group (Williams 1966; Meyers 2001).

Among the first to apply evolutionary theory to criminal behavior were Randy Thornhill and Craig T. Palmer, coauthors of *A Natural History of Rape: Biological Bases of Sexual Coercion* (2000). Drawing analogies from the sexual behavior of scorpion flies, water-striders, and other insects, Thornhill and Palmer concluded that rape is a natural biological phenomenon—a reproductive adaptation—used by men to ensue their genetic survival, which is triggered by environmental conditions or interactions in life. All men are not genetically predisposed to rape, but all men are genetically capable of rape. The more traditional and prevailing belief that rape is a social phenomenon driven by the male's desire to control and dominate females is bunk, according to Thornhill and Palmer. Thornhill and Palmer suggest the creation and implementation of a mandatory education program for both preteen males and females. The purpose of the education program for preteen males, say Thornhill and Palmer, would be to inform young males about their precondition and to teach them not to rape. Young females should be informed that all men are potential rapists, and should be instructed to take this into consideration when making decisions about their personal appearance and apparel in public. Women, who know and understand that all men are potential rapists, can avoid rape by not dressing provocatively and behaving seductively. Men, who know and understand that they have the potential to rape, can be taught not to rape, even if they are tempted by a woman's flirtatious ways. As an added deterrent, men who are unwilling to control their sexual aggressions and commit rape should be incarcerated, financially penalized and forced to take drugs and hormones that will reduce their sex drive.

As might be expected, the idea that human behavior is a product of evolution has not been received without controversy. It has prompted a storm of fiery written exchanges, in the form of books and journal articles, between supporters and critics of evolutionary psychology and sociobiology.

Notable among supporters are Richard Dawkins, Oxford University zoologist (1989); Helena Cronin, co-director of the London School of Economics Centre for Philosophy of Natural and Social Sciences (2003); Steven Pinker, professor of psychology and director of the Center for Cognitive Neuroscience at the Massachusetts Institute of Technology (2002, 1992); and Daniel Dennett, director of cognitive studies at Tufts University (1995).

Prominent critics of evolutionary psychology and sociobiology include the late Stephen Jay Gould, former paleontologist and curator for the Museum of Comparative Zoology at Harvard University (1997, 1992); Richard Lewontin, professor emeritus of zoology at Harvard University (1979); Paul Ehrlich, Bing Professor of Population Studies and president of the Center for Conservation Biology at Stanford University (2000); and Jerry Coyne, professor of ecology and evolution at the University of Chicago (2004).

Objections to Sociobiology and Evolutionary Psychology

In addition to criticism from creationists who oppose any idea about the origin of life that conflicts with the Bible, the underlying principles of sociobiology and evolutionary psychology are also criticized on political and scientific grounds.

Political objections to sociobiology and evolutionary psychology form around the concern that those who promote these concepts are motivated by a hidden agenda: to maintain the status quo and perpetuate a belief system that fosters and sustains racism, sexism, classism, and similar discriminatory ideologies and types of behavior. Critics of evolution-based theory point out that a similar attraction to genetics during the Nazi era in Germany led to the formulation and implementation of eugenic policies and practices that resulted in the annihilation of six million Jews. Others fear that wholesale adoption of the belief that behavior is genetically based may be used to reinforce the view that blacks are more predisposed to commit crime than whites—some people would explain the fact that the number of blacks arrested and convicted is disproportionately higher than that of whites because of some inherent instinct in black people, as opposed to the notion that the disparity is the product of racism.

Some black scholars, such as Alvin Poussaint, Joy DeGruy-Leary, Amy Alexander, Omar G. Reid, Sekou Mims, and Larry Higginbottom, have asserted that higher crime, unemployment, suicide, and drug-use rates among blacks are all attributable to what they have called "posttraumatic slavery syndrome."

DeGruy-Leary, assistant professor in the School of Social Work at Portland State University and self-proclaimed originator of the posttraumatic slavery syndrome theory, attributes the syndrome to traumas such as experiencing or observing serious physical harm or the threat of serious physical harm, experiencing or observing torture or a kidnapping, or witnessing a person being killed, experienced during slavery that were not properly addressed through therapy (DeGruy-Leary, 2005).

According to Alvin Poussaint, coauthor with Amy Alexander of *Lay My Burden Down: Unraveling Suicide and the Mental Health Crisis Among African-Americans* (2000), posttraumatic slavery syndrome is caused by the accumulating effects of being the victim of persistent racism, poverty, discrimination, and a lack of quality health care.

Omar G. Reid, Sekou Mims, and Larry Higginbottom—associates with Pyramid Builders, Inc., a private for-profit social service group in Roxbury, Massachusetts, (who also claim credit for developing the posttraumatic slavery theory)—argue that because black people were taught as slaves to hate themselves, it is easy for them to kill anyone who resembles them. Because black people were abused as slaves, they became abusers; and because black males were used for breeding, they never developed the ability to connect emotionally with women or children. The descendents of former slaves, according to a statement posted on the Pyramid Builders Web page (www.pyramidbuilders.org), are denied the opportunity to recover from the experiences of their forebears because "the mechanisms (academia, economic institutions, mental health, medical institutions, and government) operated by the white supremacy continue to traumatize Nubian-Americans."

Although Poussaint, DeGruy-Leary, Reid, Mims, and Higginbottom fail to adequately explain exactly how the effects of trauma experienced by slaves is transmitted to subsequent generations, DeGruy-Leary says that it is passed down in the form of adaptive behavior from one generation to another, which implies that she believes the syndrome to be genetically transmitted.

Those who object to sociobiology and evolutionary psychology on scientific grounds charge that both are pseudo-science, because the underlying theoretical constructs are not testable using empirically quantifiable data, and therefore their results are not falsifiable. Objections are also raised to the types of approach used in sociobiology and evolutionary psychology studies, as well as to the sampling and mathematical methods employed by evolutionary researchers. The approaches most commonly used by researchers to justify their position are chromosome studies, twin studies, and adoption studies.

YYX Chromosome Studies

Chromosome studies have revealed that a high number of institutionalized criminals had two Y sex-chromosomes, rather than the usual one. Researchers concluded that the extra Y-chromosome causes aggressive, antisocial, and criminal behavior.

Twin Studies

Studies involving identical twins that shared the same environmental and life experiences have led researchers to conclude that if one member of a twin set demonstrates criminal behavior and the other member of the twin set does not, the variation in behavior is caused by genetic differences, because both twins were the product of the same environmental and life experiences.

Adoption Studies

Studies of children whose biological parents had a history of criminal behavior but who were raised by a non-biologically related relative have indicated that these children were more likely to engage in criminal activity than were adopted children whose biological parents had no history of criminal behavior. In 2002, after completing a meta-analysis[4] of twin and adoption studies, Soo Hyun Rhee from the Institute of Behavior Genetics and Irwin Waldman from the Emory University department of psychology, concluded that although a person's genetic history does

---

4   See Item 3 in the Addendum for a discussion about meta-analysis, which is a somewhat controversial statistical technique.

strongly influence the manifestation of antisocial behavior, the influence of environmental factors is even stronger. Having a genetic predisposition to antisocial behavior, they say, does not necessarily result in criminal behavior on the part of the bearer unless the bearer is exposed to the necessary environmental catalysts.

John Alcock, author of *Animal Behavior: An Evolutionary Approach* and *The Triumph of Sociobiology* (2003) says that when the public learns that socio-biologists have actually been able to make good evolutionary sense of the attributes of hyenas, cowbirds, blue-footed boobies, and red-back spiders, perhaps they will become receptive to the possibility that socio-biologists have something important to say about humans as well. Dawkins 1989, Dennett 1995, and Pinker 2002 argue that behavior is determined by a gene or genes that formed through the natural selection process. Gould 1992, Lewontin 1979, and Ehrlich 2000 say that criminal behavior is not exclusively genetic in origin. Genes play a powerful role in the development of criminal behavior, but behavior in part is determined by a "spandrel," which is an unintended by-product of the natural selection process, as opposed to a gene which is created through adaptation.

The public's interest in what sociobiology has to say about human beings—if the public ever learns about sociobiology—will not be dependent, as Alcock asserts, on what sociobiology knows about hyenas, birds, spiders, and the like. The public will be interested in sociobiology only if what sociobiology has to say helps to solve the mystery of criminal behavior and eliminates the pain and suffering associated with it. The public doesn't care whether criminal behavior is a product of a gene or a spandrel. The public doesn't care whether criminal behavior stems from a combination of a gene and a spandrel. The public doesn't care whether social circumstances, psychological trauma, a brain disorder, dietary or vitamin deficiencies, or chemical imbalances cause criminal behavior. The public didn't care about the theory or science that led to Jonas Salk's development of a vaccine to prevent polio; and the public won't care about the theory or science that leads to the discovery of a cure for criminal behavior. What *is* of interest to the public is the result. Will the result prevent someone from becoming a criminal—from stealing, robbing, assaulting, raping, or killing? Argument, discussion and debate are essential ingredients to the problem-solving process; but the argument in the academic world over what causes criminal behavior and how to prevent it seems to be driven more by egotistical one-upmanship and a need for notoriety than by a need to find an answer regardless of who gets the credit. The public is not interested in or impressed with the intellectual arguments of scholars, particularly when their objective seems to be proving one another wrong rather than collaboratively working toward a solution to a common problem. This kind of argumentation may satisfy, amuse, and motivate academicians to publish and achieve tenure, but the public could not care less.

Chapter 10

EVOLUTIONISTS V. ENVIRONMENTALISTS

Although it might appear that the differences between evolutionists and environmentalists are irreconcilable, Diana Fishbein, director of the Transdisciplinary Behavioral Science Program at the Research Triangle Institute, offers an interpretation that reconciles the differences by assigning both biological and environmental circumstances vital roles in the creation of antisocial behavior (Fishbein 2000).

As Fishbein would have it, both evolutionary factors and environmental circumstances contribute to the formation of antisocial behavior, but neither one causes the behavior. Biological weaknesses determine how vulnerable an individual is to environmental circumstances. The more one's genetic makeup is compromised, the greater the probability is that one will exhibit antisocial behavior when subjected to adverse environmental circumstances.

Biological vulnerabilities, which include all of the possibilities previously discussed (defective chromosomes, malfunctions or malformations of the brain, or chemical or hormonal imbalance) make an individual vulnerable to the development of antisocial behavior. Such vulnerabilities can be either inherited or created by exposure to negative environmental conditions during both the prenatal and postnatal developmental stages.

Negative environmental conditions (such as poverty, physical and mental abuse or neglect, and prenatal exposure to drugs or alcohol) can alter one's biological mechanisms in ways that will promote antisocial behavior. Exposure to negative environmental conditions generates stress. In turn, stress alters those components of the brain that control mood, emotion, and behavior. These alterations can be either temporary or permanent. The greater the intensity and/or frequency of exposure to negative environmental conditions the greater the stress. As the level of stress increases, the probability that antisocial behavior will occur increases. Individuals who are genetically predisposed to numerous and/or severe biological deficiencies affecting the areas of the brain that control mood, emotion, and behavior are at greater risk of developing criminal behavior than those who are not similarly genetically predisposed.

Fishbein is convinced that there is no shortage of intervention strategies that could dramatically reduce the incidence of antisocial behavior. Some of the strategies extolled by Fishbein as offering the most promise are: prenatal, perinatal, and postnatal health care; cognitive-behavioral interventions; minimizing the effects of television violence; social skills training; parent training; school-based programs in intellectual enrichment, social relations, and anti-bullying; neuropsychological enhancements; cognitive remediation; problem-solving training; small-group activities with a focus on intensive behavioral rehabilitation; psycho educational programs; speech and language therapy; environmental enrichment; computer games for sensory and motor rehabilitation; functional and integrative training; interdisciplinary consultation; stress-prevention and stress-management programs; drug-cessation programs for mothers; and family therapy.

It would appear, for Fishbein's theory to work, that it would require either the elimination of stress from daily living, or the development of some method to protect the brain or stimulate it to repel the negative influences of stress—neither one of which seems likely. As was discussed earlier, stress is not a universal condition. That is, not everyone is stressed by the same things, and different people respond to stress in different ways. To protect the brain from the negative influences of stress, it would be necessary to identify every possible source of stress, determine how each person responds to each source of stress, and develop a stress-prevention strategy for each individual.

Adrian Raine, Robert G. Wright Professor of Psychology in the psychology department at the University of Southern California, believes, like Fishbein, that criminal behavior is the result of cumulative biological and sociological factors. In his book *The Psychopathology of Crime: Criminal Behavior as a Clinical Disorder* (1993), Raine argues that criminal behavior—when compared to the combined requirements of nine different definitions commonly used to define other disorders—fits the definition of a disorder as well as or better than recognized disorders such as depression or schizophrenia. When applied collectively, the nine separate definitions, says Raine, create a general gestalt or whole picture of what constitutes psychopathology. Psychopathology is a word used interchangeably by Raine with the term mental disorder.

The nine definitions used by Raine to define a disorder are: 1) Behavior that is uncommon, but deviates statistically from the norm; 2) Behavior that deviates from an ideal state of health; 3) Behavior that lies outside the bounds of social acceptability and that violates the prevailing social norm; 4) Behavior caused by suffering, psychological distress, discomfort, or unhappiness; 5) Behavior that causes a person to seek treatment; 6) Impairments in social, occupational, behavioral, educational, and cognitive functioning; 7) Behavior and accompanying diagnostic criteria outlined in the Diagnostic and Statistical Manual of Mental Disorders (DSM), which is published by the American Psychiatric Association; 8) Behavior that results from a disturbance to normal biological regulatory functions; and 9) Behavior that meets the definition of mental disorder as defined in the DSM which is "a clinically significant behavioral or psychological syndrome that is associated with distress or an increased risk of suffering death, pain, disability, or an important loss of freedom that is considered to be a manifestation of a behavioral, psychological or biological dysfunction in the person, not a response to a specific isolated event."

The following table, created by Raine, reflects his subjective assessment of the extent to which criminal behavior and three other recognized disorders meet the criteria of the nine different definitions.

Table 9: Definitions of Mental Disorder

Definition	Criminal Behavior	Schizotypical Personality	Schizophrenia	Caffeine Intoxication
Statistical Deviation	Moderate	Moderate	Good	Poor
Ideal Health	Good	Good	Good	Poor
Deviation from Social Norm	Good	Moderate	Good	Poor
Distress and Suffering	Moderate	Poor	Good	Moderate
Seeks Treatment	Poor	Poor	Moderate	Poor
Impaired Functioning	Good	Moderate	Good	Poor
Listing in DSM	Good	Good	Good	Good
Biological Functioning	Moderate	Moderate	Good	Poor
Defined in DSM	Good	Good	Good	Poor

The utility of Raine's theory for solving the mystery of criminal behavior, like Fishbein's theory, is dependent on the validity and acceptance of the sociological and biological theory, which has yet to be decided. More basically, and perhaps more importantly, the usefulness of Raine's theory depends on whether a subjective definition of a disorder—constructed by selectively merging features of multiple definitions, as well as the subjective application of the final definition to criminal behavior—can be objectively validated.

If Raine's contention that criminal behavior is a disorder were to be objectively validated, it would suggest that massive change would be necessary in how society responds to criminal behavior. Accepting criminal behavior as a disorder would establish that criminal offenders are not responsible for their behavior, which would create a series of unanswered questions about how society can protect law-abiding citizens without violating an offender's right to treatment. If criminal behavior were classified as a disorder, could criminals be arrested and confined against their will as they are now? Could they reject treatment, which is currently the prerogative of anyone diagnosed with a mental disorder? Could a person being victimized use physical or lethal force to protect him or herself? Could a law-enforcement officer use physical or lethal force to prevent a criminal act? Could victims expect to be financially compensated for personal injury or property loss? The answers to these questions would have a profound impact on the shape and administration of the criminal justice system.

Part 3

Obstacles to Solving the Mystery of Criminal Behavior

Humanity is confronted every day with mysteries of various sorts. Some mysteries, such as how to predict the weather accurately, are relatively mundane. Other mysteries, such as those involving missing persons, murders or the cure for a major health problem, are not so mundane. But all mysteries have one thing in common: they present a unique set of obstacles that must be overcome before the mystery can be solved. There are at least three obstacles that must be overcome before the mystery of criminal behavior can be solved: 1) pseudoscientific research practices; 2) prisons; and 3) intellectual and ideological parochialism.

Chapter 11

PSEUDOSCIENTIFIC RESEARCH PRACTICES

In 1967, the Commission on Law Enforcement and Administration of Justice, appointed by President Lyndon Johnson, concluded that the failure to conduct systematic research and evaluation had put the criminal justice system in the embarrassing situation of being unable to even know when programs were successful or unsuccessful. As a result, the commission said that programs had been repetitiously continued and/or expanded based on unproven theories. The commission referred to this process as "intuitive opportunism or goal-oriented guessing."

In 1996, nearly thirty years after the commission published its report, the United States Congress mandated the Attorney General to commission an independent comprehensive evaluation of the effectiveness of programs that had been designed and administered by state and local law enforcement agencies and communities to prevent crime and that were funded in whole or in part by federal grants. The total amount of money allocated to such programs exceeds three billion dollars annually.

After an extensive search directed by the National Institute of Justice, the University of Maryland's Department of Criminology and Criminal Justice was selected to conduct the evaluation. Members of this faculty did not actually evaluate the effectiveness of each program, rather they evaluated the methods used in over five hundred crime-prevention studies, using a rating scale to determine the degree to which the methodology used in a particular study had met generally accepted standards expected in scientific research. Each study was given a numerical rating, ranging from one to five. The higher the score, the more confidence the authors of the report assigned to the validity of the findings and the conclusions of a particular study. After receiving a numerical score, each study was assigned to one of three classes: programs that work; programs that don't work; and programs that show promise. Rather than categorizing crime-prevention programs as classical or positivist, the authors of *Preventing Crime: What Works, What Doesn't What's Promising*,[5] divided programs into seven categories (Sherman et al. 1996).

---

5   See Item 4 in the Addendum for a discussion about international approaches to crime prevention studies.

Community-Based Crime Prevention Programs

Community-based crime prevention programs are those designed and implemented by local community leaders. Examples include volunteer mentoring and gun buyback programs.

Family-Based Crime Prevention Programs

The objective of family-based crime prevention programs is to reduce the incidence of child abuse, domestic violence, and poor parenting, which are all factors thought to promote criminal behavior.

School-Based Crime Prevention Programs

School-based crime prevention programs are those directed at students who demonstrate behavior indicative of early delinquency, such as a lack of interest in school activities, poor academic performance, behavior problems, and poor attendance.

Labor-Market Crime Prevention Programs

The underlying premise of labor-market-related crime prevention programs is that crime is the product of an interaction between individuals with both the propensity to commit crime and the opportunity to commit crime. High unemployment, according to this theory, increases the propensity and opportunity for crime; and low unemployment decreases them.

Crime Prevention Programs in Places

Crime prevention programs in places are programs designed to reduce crime in places where the rate of crime is high by making it more difficult to commit a crime, enhancing the possibility of being caught, and making crime less rewarding. "Places" are defined in the report as very small areas reserved for a narrow range of functions, often controlled by a single owner, and separated from the surrounding area—places such as stores, homes, apartment buildings, street corners, subway stations, airports, and buses.

Police Crime-Prevention Programs

Police crime-prevention programs are those designed on the basis of one or more of the following hypotheses: 1) The more police a city employs, the less crime will occur; 2) The faster police respond to a crime scene, the less crime will occur; 3) Random police patrols in public places result in less crime; 4) Police patrols targeted at specific locations at times when crime is most often committed will prevent crime at those specific times and locations; 5) The more arrests police make in response to reported crimes of all types, the less crime will occur; 6) The more arrests police make for serious violent crimes committed by high-risk offenders, the less serious crime will occur; 7) Increasing the quantity of police present in the community and improving the quality of the interaction between the police and citizens in the community will result in less crime; and 8) The more police can identify and minimize the causes of specific crime patterns, the less crime will occur.

Criminal-Justice Crime Prevention Programs

Criminal-justice crime prevention programs are those used by courts and corrections services to reduce the criminal activities of offenders who have already been convicted of a crime, as opposed to those not yet involved in crime.

Programs that Work

Of the more than five hundred studies evaluated by the University of Maryland faculty, only thirteen programs were found to be effective in preventing crime: three family-based programs; three school-based programs; one labor-market-based program; one place-based program; two police-based programs; and three criminal-justice-based programs.

- Family-based programs that worked were long-term, frequent home visits (by professional service providers skilled in the identified problem area) combined with participation in preschool events, which are shown to prevent delinquency; weekly visits to homes with infants, which have been shown to reduce child abuse and injuries; and family therapy by clinical staff for delinquent and pre-delinquent youth.

- School-based programs that worked included those aimed at building schools' capability to initiate and sustain innovation; programs aimed at clarifying and communicating norms about behavior, with an emphasis on positive reinforcement; and comprehensive instructional programs that focused on developing social competency and thinking skills such as self-control, decision-making, problem-solving, and communication skills.

- The only labor-market-based program that was found to work was a short-term vocational training program for older male ex-offenders who were no longer involved in the criminal justice system.

- The sole crime prevention program for places that met the study's standards was the implementation of nuisance-abatement control measures directed at controlling drug-dealing and related crime at private rental places.

- The two police-based prevention programs identified as working were increased police patrols at specific locations at times when crimes were most often committed; and the proactive arrests of serious repeat offenders and drunk drivers.

- Criminal-justice-based programs identified as successful included rehabilitation programs with particular characteristics (successful rehabilitation programs being characterized as those that utilize multiple treatment components with a structured focus on developing social, academic, and employment coping skills, and that use cognitive restructuring methods to change clearly-identified overt and undesirable behaviors associated with the offender's criminal activities, as opposed to nondirective counseling focused on insight and self-esteem issues); prison-based therapeutic community substance-abuse programs that operated as a twenty-four-hour live-in facilities within prisons; and the extended incarceration of offenders who continue to commit crimes at high rates.

Two primary conclusions were drawn from the study: first, substantial reductions in national rates of serious crime can only be achieved by prevention in areas of concentrated poverty, where the majority of all homicides in the nation occur and where homicide rates are twenty times the national average; and second, most crime prevention is the result of informal and formal practices and programs that take place in the seven named institutional settings. All seven institutional settings appear to be interdependent. Events which occur in one institution can affect events in other institutions. Collectively, these events can affect crime rates, which suggests, according to the report, that effective crime prevention may require simultaneous investment in programs in multiple institutions.

In addition to these two primary conclusions, the results of the report also support at least one other major conclusion: the finding of President Johnson's 1967 Commission on Law Enforcement and Administration of Justice that failure to conduct systematic research and evaluation had put the criminal justice system in the embarrassing situation of being unable to even know even when programs were successful or unsuccessful was still true nearly thirty years later.

There should be no dispute over the fact that most of the research that has been conducted to test the validity of theories about criminal behavior and crime prevention has failed to apply the rigorous methods required of legitimate scientific investigation. The literature is replete with results of research and evaluation studies completed on a vast array of different crime prevention programs; but most of the research and evaluation was not systematically conducted, and the results of the vast majority of these studies are invalid and unreliable because the methods used to conduct them failed to comply with the standards required in a scientific inquiry.

What is commonly overlooked, however, is that research involving human subjects is highly scrutinized and tightly controlled by government regulations and ethical standards self-imposed by researchers—significantly more so than research not involving human subjects. In the United States, both the federal government and most state governments have codified laws and promulgated regulations to govern human-subject research. Similar regulations have been adopted in many foreign countries. In addition to government regulation, every reputable public and private university and research institution, and every professional discipline engaged in human-subject research, has voluntarily adopted ethical standards of practice to govern the conduct of all persons involved in such research. The intent of these regulations and standards is to protect the rights of participants, and to ensure that they have not been coerced into participating. As will be discussed below, the regulations and standards are even more stringent if the subjects of the research are prisoners—so stringent that it may be impossible to conduct the research necessary to find a solution to the mystery of criminal behavior.

Title 45 of the Code of Federal Regulations, Part 46, "Protection of Human Subjects," was adopted and has been administered by the United States Department of Health and Human Services, the National Institutes of Health, and the Office for Protection from Research Risks. These particular regulations apply to all research involving human subjects that is conducted or supported by any federal department or agency, as well as human-subject research that is conducted by an agency or individual that is subject to regulation by any federal department or agency in the United States. The application of these regulations also extends to research conducted outside the United States if the research conducted is supported by or subject to regulation by any federal department or agency of the United States government.

A human subject, as defined in these regulations, is a living individual about whom an investigator (whether professional or student) conducting research obtains data or identifiable private information through intervention or interaction with the individual. Intervention includes both physical procedures and manipulation of the subject's environment. Interaction includes communication or interpersonal contact between the investigator and the subject. Private information is information about behavior that occurs in a context in which an individual can reasonably expect that no observation or recording is taking place, as well as information the individual can reasonably expect will not be made public, such as medical records.

Procedurally, the regulations require each institution (meaning any public or private entity) governed by them to establish an Institutional Review Board (IRB). The responsibility of an IRB is to review and approve all research proposals involving human subjects, in order to ensure that the proposal satisfies all regulatory requirements and includes adequate provisions to protect the rights and welfare of human subjects. The IRB must have at least five members with varying backgrounds and sufficient expertise and experience in their fields to promote respect for the IRB's decisions. At least one of the IRB members must have a scientific background and one must have a background in a nonscientific area. In addition, an IRB may install an ad hoc member to assist the IRB in its deliberations regarding issues that fall outside the areas of expertise of the standing members.

Prisoners are considered a vulnerable category of subjects, along with children, pregnant women, and people with mental or physical disabilities. Prisoners are considered vulnerable because the constraints of incarceration could affect their ability to make a truly voluntary and non-coerced decision regarding whether or not to participate in the research. The definition of a prisoner included in the regulations is broadly written; it not only refers to any individual involuntarily confined or detained in a penal institution for a criminal or civil crime, but also includes those detained in other facilities that provide alternatives to criminal prosecution or incarceration in a penal institution, as well as individuals detained pending arraignment, trial, or sentencing.

When considering a research proposal involving prisoners, an IRB must include at least one prisoner or prisoner representative who has the appropriate background and expertise to serve in that capacity. The remaining members of the board must have no outside affiliation with prisons. Biomedical and behavioral research, which would be among the most likely forms of research with prisoners, is held to a higher standard than other forms of research. Authorization for biomedical or behavioral research involving prisoners that is conducted or supported by the Department of Human and Health Services (DHHS) requires not only the approval of an IRB, but also that of the DHHS secretary. To authorize biomedical or behavioral research, the DHHS secretary must conclude, after reviewing the proposal, that the research is limited to the following categories:

- Studies of the possible causes, effects, and processes of incarceration and criminal behavior, with the study presenting no more than minimal risk and no more than inconvenience to the participants.

- Studies of prisons as institutional structures or prisoners as incarcerated persons, provided that the study presents no more minimal risk and no more than inconvenience to the participants.

- Research on conditions that particularly affect prisoners as a class, such as hepatitis, alcoholism, drug addiction, and sexual assaults—but only after the secretary has consulted with experts in penology, medicine, and ethics, and has published a notice of intent to approve in the *Federal Register*.

- Research which has the intent and reasonable probability of improving the health or welfare of the participants.

- Research that requires the assignment of prisoners to a control group in which the prisoners are not likely to benefit, but not until the Secretary has consulted with appropriate experts, including those in penology, medicine, and ethics, and has published a notice of intent to approve in the *Federal Register*.

Ultimately, an IRB is empowered to: 1) approve a proposal; 2) require modifications before approval; or 3) disapprove a proposal. To approve a proposal, the IRB must determine that all of the following requirements are satisfied:

- Risks to the participants must be minimized in two ways. First, the procedures being used must be consistent with sound research design and must not unnecessarily expose the participants to risk. Second, the procedures being used must, when appropriate, be the same procedures being used on the participants for diagnostic and treatment purposes.

- Risks to participants must be minimal relative to any anticipated benefits that may be derived by the participants and the importance of the knowledge expected to be learned. "Minimal risk" means that the probability and magnitude of harm or discomfort to the participants must be no greater than the magnitude of harm or discomfort that would be expected as a result of receiving a physical or psychological examination or test in ordinary daily life.

- Selection of the participants must be equitable, taking into the account the purpose of the research, the setting in which it will be conducted, and any special problems the research may pose for the participants if they are a member of one of the vulnerable categories.

- Informed consent must be obtained from each participant or the participant's legally authorized representative, and this consent must be properly documented. When informed consent is sought, the following information must be provided to each prospective participant:

  - A statement acknowledging that the study involves research, an explanation of the study's purpose and expected duration, a description of the procedures involved, and a clear identification of any procedures that are experimental.

  - A description of any foreseeable risks or discomforts.

  - A description of any benefits the participant or others might expect from the research.

  - Disclosure of any alternative procedures or treatment approaches.

  - A statement describing how the confidentiality of the records will be maintained.

- If the anticipated risk is more than minimal, information about any compensation or medical after-care that would be available should an injury occur, and instructions as to how these benefits would be obtained.

- Information about whom to contact, and how to contact them, if the participant has questions regarding the research, participant rights, or a research-related injury.

- A statement that participation is voluntary, that refusal to participate must not result in any loss of benefits to which the participant is otherwise entitled and that the participant may withdraw at anytime without penalty.

Once approval has been granted to conduct research involving human subjects, the rigorous standards of the scientific method still need to be satisfied. To satisfy these requirements, experiments must be designed and conducted in accordance with a multi-step protocol that must be carefully regimented.

Conducting scientific experiments on primates for the benefit of humans is legal and socially acceptable within limits, although it does encounter protest. Conducting scientific research on human beings is theoretically legal; but it is extremely difficult—justifiably so—because of the safeguards built into the protocols governing this type of research. These safeguards are necessary to prevent abuse and to guarantee the rigors of the scientific method, which are essential if researchers are to ensure that their results are objective and valid. Research practices can and must be elevated beyond the level of "intuitive opportunism or goal-oriented guessing," which the vast majority of research conducted to date has not been. The achievement of a higher level of research practice will require much greater diligence and discipline on the part of researchers. They must ensure compliance with the protocols governing research on human beings, and meet the requirements of the scientific method. Failure to do so will perpetuate pseudoscientific research that will continue to produce results which contribute little or nothing toward discovering what causes criminal behavior and how to prevent it. Without better research, corrections policy and practice will continue to be based on myths, intuition, and the prerogatives of power.

Chapter 12

PRISONS

Whenever the topic of corrections is discussed by politicians or reviewed by the press, prisons dominate the discussion. The vast majority of studies and scholarly writing appear to focus on prisons. Exactly why prisons garner so much attention is unclear, but there are a number of possible reasons. One, prisons are an imposing edifice, used by the entertainment industry and the news media, both electronic and print, as a symbol for punishment. Two, prisons consume a huge amount of financial resources that law-abiding citizens argue should be more appropriately spent on education, health care, and other forms of human services. Three, prisons are an environmentally friendly, pollution-free industry that creates jobs. It is not uncommon, when a government announces plans to build a new prison, for towns and cities to compete to have it located in their community. In 2003, the prison systems operated by the fifty states and the federal government had a combined workforce of 498,362, and a combined operating budget in excess of $60 billion—between 60 and 70 percent of which paid for wages and benefits (Stephen 2004; Hughes 2006; Office of Management and Budget 2006). Eliminating or reducing the use of prisons would put thousands of people out of work.

Multiple proposals, too numerous to count, have been advanced over the years to reform prisons. Generally, prison-reform proposals are centered on one of two philosophies: would-be reformers either argue that prisons are too luxurious and promote modifications that would make them more austere, or they argue that prisons are virtual dungeons, and propose changes that would make them more humane.

One of the most recent calls for prison reform, which falls into the latter category, was spawned in August 2003 by United States Supreme Court Justice Anthony M. Kennedy. In a speech at the American Bar Association's (ABA's) annual meeting, Justice Kennedy chastised the legal profession for focusing too much on the process of determining guilt and innocence, and paying too little attention to what happens after a prisoner is put away in prison. In addition to being troubled by the large number of people who are sent to prison, Kennedy expressed concern for the disproportionate impact of incarceration on minorities, the cost and length of incarceration, sentencing guidelines[6] and mandatory minimum sentences, the

---

6   See Item 5 in the Addendum for a discussion about sentencing guidelines—standards developed in the late 1980s to reduce disparity in the length of prison terms imposed by the courts.

importance of judicial discretion in sentencing, the atrophy of the pardon power, the dehumanizing experience of prison, and the importance of rehabilitation as a punishment goal. In Justice Kennedy's view, the resources of the criminal justice system are misspent, its punishments are too severe, and its sentences are too long. He challenged the ABA to help start a new public discussion about the prison system (Kennedy 2003).

In response to Justice Kennedy's challenge, the bar association appointed a Commission to study Justice Kennedy's concerns. In August 2004, this commission issued a report of its findings in the form of five resolutions (American Bar Association, 2004).

Resolution #1: The American Bar Association urges states, territories, and the federal government to ensure that prisoners are effectively supervised in safe, secure environments; that correctional staff are properly trained and supervised; and that allegations of mistreatment are promptly investigated and are dealt with swiftly and appropriately.

Resolution #2: The American Bar Association urges states, territories, and the federal government to prepare prisoners for release back into the community by implementing policies and programs that from the beginning of incarceration provide appropriate programming, including substance-abuse treatment, educational and job training opportunities, and mental-health counseling and services; and encourage prisoner participation by giving credit toward satisfaction of sentences for successful completion of such programs.

Resolution #3: The American Bar Association urges states, territories, and the federal government to assist prisoners who have been released into the community by implementing policies and programs that establish community partnerships that include corrections, police, prosecutors, and community representatives committed to promoting successful reentry into the community and that measure their performance by the overall success of reentry; and assist prisoners returning to the community with transitional housing, job-placement assistance, and substance-abuse avoidance.

Resolution #4: The American Bar Association urges states, territories, and the federal government, in order to remove unwarranted legal barriers to reentry, to identify collateral sanctions imposed upon conviction and discretionary disqualification of convicted persons from other generally available opportunities and benefits; limit collateral sanctions to those that are specifically warranted by the conduct underlying the conviction, and prohibit those that unreasonably infringe on fundamental rights or frustrate successful reentry; and limit situations in which a convicted person may be disqualified from otherwise available benefits and opportunities, including employment, to the greatest extent consistent with public safety.

Resolution #5: The American Bar Association urges law schools to establish reentry clinics in which students assist individuals who have been imprisoned and are seeking to reestablish themselves in the community to regain legal rights or remove collateral disabilities.

Both Justice Kennedy's concerns and the bar association's resolutions represent a reinvention and re-presentation of vintage views that have previously been advanced by earlier reformers; and are predicated on the assumption that academic education, job training, and guidance counseling in prison—followed by equal employment opportunity in the community after release—will stop criminals from re-offending. Past efforts to reform prisons, based on the same or very similar principles as those espoused by Justice Kennedy and the bar association, provided no new insight into what causes criminal behavior or how to prevent it; and it is unlikely that any renewed effort to reform prisons—based on these same ideas—will do any better.

Although some assert that prisons can be converted into therapeutic communities—or at least that therapeutic communities can be created within prisons—the guiding philosophies and operating principles of a therapeutic community, when contrasted with the guiding philosophies and operating principles of a prison, reveal that a therapeutic community is in fact the antithesis of a prison (Kennard 1998; Campling and Haigh 1999; DeLeon 2000).

Admission to a therapeutic community is typically voluntary, as is the decision to leave. This is not so with a prison. People are placed in prison involuntarily, and might be killed if they attempt to leave before they are authorized to leave. The population of a therapeutic community is intentionally kept small (usually between fifteen and thirty people) to promote the development of interpersonal relationships between staff and residents, and among the residents themselves. Prisons are designed to hold large numbers of people (the population of a prison can range from one hundred to three thousand). The large size of a prison's population is hardly conducive to the formulation of supportive and mutually beneficial relationships among the prisoners, or between the prisoners and those who watch over them.

In a true therapeutic community, there is no difference in status between staff and residents; they are all considered to be members of a kind of family. In a prison, fraternization between inmates and staff is, by rule, prohibited.

Employees who violate this rule are subject to discipline, up to and including termination. "Firm but fair" are the watchwords in most prisons. Residents of a therapeutic community share in the development of the rules of conduct as well as in the imposition of discipline when the rules are broken, and in the granting of rewards for good conduct. In most prisons, these functions and activities are decided by the staff. (Some states, e.g., Oregon, Washington, and Wisconsin, have adopted administrative processes that permit inmates to have some input into the content of rules of conduct and other procedures that directly affect them. The process requires only that the inmates input "be considered," and may have no impact on the final outcome.)

Peer pressure is considered one of the strongest motivators to change in a therapeutic community and is encouraged. Residents participate in making job assignments, granting promotions, and awarding other community privileges. Preservation of individual identity is promoted by allowing residents of a therapeutic community to wear civilian clothing of their own choice. Prison rules and operating procedures are, by design, intended to promote uniformity within the inmate population and to prevent any inmate from influencing the behavior of another inmate or having any control over the activity of another inmate.

In prison, someone in authority makes almost every decision for a prisoner. Someone other than the prisoners determine: the sleep schedule; what clothing can be worn; when to shower; when and what to eat; when and where to work; who may visit; when and where they may visit; how long a visit can last, and how frequently visits may occur. Meals for those in the general population are typically served cafeteria-style three times daily in a large dining room not unlike a school cafeteria, except that the tables and stools are bolted to the floor. Depending on the size of the prison population, it may take up to three hours to serve a single meal to the entire population, and each inmate may be allowed no more than fifteen minutes to consume a meal. In a prison, the concept of privacy is, for inmates, just a memory. Prisoners typically bathe in group showers similar to those in school locker rooms. Clothing is centrally laundered and exchanged once per week, unless a prisoner is working at a job that requires more frequent clothing exchange.

Most of the prison population goes about its daily schedule (work, school, recreation, medical appointments) without incident. There is a percentage of the prison population, however, that continues to engage in criminal activity by stealing, robbing, assaulting, raping, or even murdering other prisoners or staff. To prevent weaker prisoners from being abused, tormented, harassed, physically assaulted, or compelled to pay for protection or share their private property with more aggressive prisoners, the architecture and operation of prisons are in part designed to ensure that no prisoner has influence or control over another prisoner. Those prisoners who break institutional rules or commit crimes are confined to the prison jail, commonly called a segregation unit. In the segregation unit, a prisoner, depending on how dangerous he or she is, may be confined to a cell for up to twenty-three hours per day, being allowed out of the cell for no more than one hour to shower and exercise. If a prisoner in segregation poses a serious threat to others, he or she may be placed in leg irons and shackles before their cell door is opened.

As previously discussed, most criminals are by nature impulsive, manipulative, and deceitful. They typically act without forethought or planning; fail to consider the consequences of actions or the impact their actions may have on others. They have no regard for rules, moral standards, laws, or the rights and property of others; and, they find it difficult to establish and maintain interpersonal relationships or to show remorse or concern for others. Given the type of behavior that most criminals manifest, it is illogical to think that confining hundreds—sometimes thousands—in the limited confines of a prison would be or could be a therapeutic experience. The environment in a prison lends itself more to reinforcing criminal values, than it does to diminishing them. Lawrence W. Sherman, a member of the faculty at the University of Maryland and coauthor of the report *What Works?*, observed in this report that the philosophy of empowering community leaders to design and implement their own crime prevention strategies may amount to throwing people overboard and then letting them design their own life preservers. Sherman's observation would seem equally fitting to the idea that prisons can be turned into therapeutic communities.

In addition to considering prisons as therapeutic communities, attributing a criminal's failure after release from prison to what a prisoner did or did not do while in prison implies that changing behavior is a procedure; it ignores the influences of outside forces and individual responsibility, and it creates false expectations in the minds of public about what results are reasonable to expect when a person is incarcerated. Changing the behavior of any person, criminal or non-criminal is not a procedure it is a process that typically requires a prolonged period of time. In the case of an incarcerated criminal, the change process may start upon admission to prison, but it does not end upon release. Normally, the process of change must continue long after a criminal is released, and long after the prison relinquishes control over him or her.

It may be that the effectiveness of prison programs[7] could be improved if the programs could impose warranties similar to those issued by automobile manufactures. Such warranties are contingent upon certain conditions being met: the oil, transmission fluid, or engine coolant, for example, must be changed at specified intervals. If a mechanical failure occurs and the conditions of the warranty have not been observed, the owner is responsible for the failure, not the manufacture. If a prison could issue a warranty which required that upon release from prison, an ex-offender must be guaranteed a job, housing, medical assistance, and other support services or the warranty is otherwise void, then more prisoners might be successful after release. Absent such a warranty, the only thing that can be expected with some certainty by putting a criminal in prison is that the individual will not commit any further crimes while incarcerated, except for those that might be committed against other prisoners or prison staff.

---

7   See Item 6 in the Addendum for a discussion about the two most commonly used criteria for measuring the effectiveness of crime prevention programs, crime rates and recidivism rates.

Over the years, the design and structure of prisons have been modified—buildings have replaced stockades, fences have replaced walls, and cell-blocks are now called "pods." The word "prison" was replaced with the word "penitentiary," which has been dropped in favor of "correctional center," "reformatory," or "correctional institution." Even the label placed on occupants of prisons has changed from "convict," to "prisoner," to "inmate," to "resident," to even "client." Tom Gaddis, author of *The Birdman of Alcatraz,* referred to this word-game as a "semantic mantel," by which he meant that labels were changed to reflect progress, enlightenment, improvement, when in reality no substantive change had occurred at all. No matter what its design or structure, no matter what its name, and no matter what its occupants are called, a prison remains a prison.

While other fields and disciplines in the modern world are developing new ways of using high-tech knowledge to improve their practices, the field of corrections is not. Consider the following brief sampling of widely accepted adaptations of technology that have increased the effectiveness of human endeavors in other fields: laser surgery, computerized x-rays, arthroscopic surgery, robotic assembly, computerized drafting, and laser-guided weapons systems. In contrast to medical services, manufacturing, and military defense, America's corrections system continues to rely almost exclusively on traditional probation programs and some form of a prison to control criminals. Infrared, microwave and fiber-optic technologies are being used to improve prison perimeter control systems; computers are sometimes used to automate inmate count; and robotic sentries are available (although not heavily utilized). In contrast to other fields, the development and application of new technologies in corrections is almost unobservable.

One form of new technology that holds great potential for improving the ability of corrections to monitor and control the whereabouts of criminal offenders in the community and perhaps could be used as a true alternative to prison is surgically implanted transponders monitored by satellites. The use of electronic monitoring systems has been suggested by others. Ralph K. Schwitzgebel was an early proponent:

> Properly used electronic technology could extend the rights of recidivists or mental patients by facilitating their early return to greater freedom in the community. In fact, when specific offending behaviors can be predicted or regulated in the community, prisons may no longer be necessary to control illegal behavior and protect the public alike. (Schwitzgebel 1969, p. 598)

Charles M. Friel, Joseph B. Vaughn, and Rolando del Carmen urge a more cautious approach:

> Electronic monitoring can be a useful tool in the repertoire of criminal justice control strategies: however … [t]hose who require extended periods of continuous surveillance probably belong in an institution and not in the community. (Friel, Vaughn, and del Carmen 1986, p viii)

Transponders installed in a bracelet or anklet is currently in wide use in the United States and some European countries. Such devices help pinpoint the location of an offender, as long as the anklet or bracelet is not removed. Once the anklet or bracelet is removed, however, it is of no use helping to locate the missing offender. Requiring sex offenders, rapists, or other predatory criminals to register with local law enforcement, and to publicize their addresses to the community, serves no useful purpose, if those accountable for monitoring and controlling the whereabouts of the offender have no way of knowing the offender's location at all times. To know the location of an offender at any given moment requires the use of a new approach, such as surgically implanted transponders.

Unlike an electronic anklet or bracelet, a surgically implanted transponder could not be easily removed or deactivated by the offender. A surgically implanted transponder, constantly monitored by a satellite surveillance system, would immediately alert authorities if an offender left an authorized area without permission and allow authorities to track and apprehend the offender.

Surgically implanted transponders tracked by a satellite surveillance system could be used to gain better control over criminals on probation or parole, and have the potential to allow some criminals currently confined in prisons to live in their own homes or other privately or publicly owned and operated residential facilities, which would be significantly less costly to build and operate than traditional prisons. Attempts at rehabilitation could be conducted in the community utilizing resources already available, thus obviating the need to duplicate such resources inside a prison, and making it no longer necessary to try to convert a prison into a therapeutic community.

Comparatively speaking, the cost of monitoring and controlling criminals using surgical implants and a satellite surveillance system would be significantly less than that of operating the existing prison system. In 2003, the fifty states spent $38.4 billion on correctional services. Over half of that money was spent to operate state prisons. In addition, the Federal Bureau of Prisons spent nearly $4 billion to operate federal prisons, and local governments spent about $10 billion to operate jails (Hughes 2006). The average daily cost of incarceration in 2004 was reported to be $62/inmate (Stephens, 2004). The average daily cost for supervising a probationer in 2000 was reported to vary from $4/day to $40/day depending on the level of supervision a probationer requires (Shilton 2000).

A system of satellites capable of tracking mobile transponders is already in orbit around the earth. The system is currently used extensively by the military, the transportation industry, and for recreational purposes by hikers, hunters, and other outdoor enthusiasts. Implanted microchips are currently being used to identify exotic animals and to assist in their recovery when stolen. In October 2004, the United States Food and Drug Administration (FDA) approved the use of the world's first radio-frequency identification chip for humans. Developed by Digital Angel Corporation, the Verichip, which is about the size of a grain of rice, can be inserted by syringe under a person's skin for an estimated cost of $150 to $200. Once inserted, the chip is undetectable by the human eye. A number of private sector companies have been formed to provide tracking services. The cost for tracking criminals outfitted with an electronic anklet or bracelet has been advertised for as low as $8.75/day.

As radical as it may sound, efforts to reform prisons should be abandoned in favor of efforts to replace them. Prison should not be replaced because they are either too lenient or cruel and inhumane as reformers argue. Prisons should be replaced because they represent an antiquated concept that operate on what should now be acknowledged is a questionable premise—punishment is an effective deterrent and behavior modifier. Continuing efforts to reform prisons only serves to perpetuate their existence and serves as a major obstacle to the possible discovery of what causes criminal behavior and how to prevent it.

Chapter 13

INTELLECTUAL AND IDEOLOGICAL PAROCHIALISM

Samuel Yochelson and Stanton Samenow—pioneers in the development of cognitive therapy—maintain that knowing the cause of criminal behavior is unimportant. This may be true if one's objective is limited to teaching those criminals who are caught how to avoid further criminal activity; but knowing what causes criminal behavior is essential if one's objective is to prevent criminal behavior before it manifests itself.

The first step toward solving a problem, after it has been recognized, is to accurately define it. Failure to accurately define a problem will result in solutions that don't work.

The second step toward solving a problem is to identify its cause(s). Identifying the symptoms of a problem is of little value in developing a solution. To develop a solution, the root cause(s) for the problem must be identified. Failure to accurately identify the cause(s) of a problem will result in the formulation of remedies or solutions that are doomed to failure. In an automobile, the symptoms of poor engine performance caused by a defect in the fuel system can be quite similar to the symptoms of poor performance caused by a malfunction in the electrical system; but replacing or repairing the carburetor of an automobile will not solve a performance problem caused by a malfunctioning electrical system. Similar symptoms in medicine, if treated universally, can have fatal consequences. Fever, shivering, chills, malaise, loss of appetite, and body aches and pains are symptoms that can indicate that the body is reacting to an infection. Because influenza is the most common infection indicative of these symptoms, they are commonly referred to as "flu like." These same symptoms, however, are also indicative of HIV infection, viral hepatitis, food poisoning, lymphoma, leukemia, and many different infectious viral diseases. Treating any of these diseases as the flu will result in failure and the possible death of the patient.

The third step in the problem-solving process is to identify possible solutions. All too often, researchers involved in the investigation of criminal behavior abbreviate the problem-solving process by pausing at, or skipping entirely, the first and second steps in the process, and moving directly to step three. Formulating a solution before a problem has been accurately defined and before the cause(s) of the problem have been correctly identified may accidentally result in a solution that works, but the probability is significantly greater that it will not.

Some scholars claim to know what causes crime and how to prevent it. Generally, these people blame the public, the media, politicians and/or special interest groups who, they assert, have a financial interest in maintaining the status quo.

Gloria Laycock says that the confidence held by politicians, the media, and the public in punitive sanctions is misplaced, because crime policy is determined by intuition, anecdote, perceived wisdom, and untutored wisdom rather than by the results of science. To improve the situation, Laycock calls for a change in the working relationship between politicians and academicians. She says that politicians need to demand that academicians address the problem of crime reduction directly, and develop reliable, clear-cut solutions based on scientific evidence; and that academicians must expand their audience and publish the results of their work in forums beyond the of obscure journals. Laycock believes that until these things happen, the media, politicians, and, in turn, the public will remain focused on punishing criminals rather than preventing crime.

There is ample justification to support Laycock's conclusion that crime policy is determined by intuition, anecdote, perceived wisdom and untutored wisdom; and it may be that the broader distribution of academic findings will redirect the alleged focus of the media, politicians, and public away from punishment and toward less punitive sanctions; but this will not happen until more proven, reliable results that support alternative approaches become available.

Matthew Robinson, a professor of criminology and criminal justice at Appalachian State University, has devised what he calls an "integrated systems theory of antisocial behavior" to explain the etiology of criminal behavior (Robinson 2004). Robinson devised his theory by reviewing the results of a variety of research projects and selecting risk factors that contribute to the development of criminal behavior that he believes have been "scientifically validated by empirical evidence." According to Robinson, all behavior, including antisocial (criminal) behavior is "the outcome of [multiple] factors interacting at ... the cell level, organ level, organism level, group level, organization/community level and society level," (p.32) and a cause-and-effect relationship can never be demonstrated when it comes to human behavior.

The operative word in Robinson's theory is "interacting." Exposure to a single risk factor does not promote antisocial behavior; nor, necessarily, does exposure to multiple risk factors. Manifestation of antisocial (or criminal) behavior, according to Robinson, is dependent upon the frequency, intensity, and priority of a person's exposure.

Because all individuals are different in their biological behavior and social experiences, [risk] factors affect people differently.... [T]he effects of the risk factors on behavior will depend on the frequency, regularity, intensity, and priority of a person's exposure, so that the more times a person is exposed (frequency), the more consistently one is exposed (regularity), the earlier a person is exposed (priority), and the stronger the factor (intensity), the more likely antisocial behavior will occur (p. 271).

The critical risk factors identified by Robinson include genetics, maternal drug use/abuse, maternal diet/nutrition, stress during pregnancy, exposure to environmental toxins, diet/nutrition, family influences, neurotransmitters/enzymes, brain dysfunction, verbal IQ/cognition, hormones, drug use/abuse, mental illness, peer influences, strain, destructive labeling, employment problems, and relationship problems.

The following table developed by Robinson (p.270) reflects how he perceives the risk factors interact to develop antisocial behavior:

Table 10: Antisocial Risk Factors

Prebirth/Birth Early Childhood Adolescence Early Adulthood

Genetics ————————————————————»

Maternal drug use/abuse ———————————————»

Maternal diet/nutrition ———————————————»

Stress during pregnancy ———————————————»

Exposure to environmental toxins ————————————»

    Diet/nutrition ———————————————»

    Family influences ———————————————»

    Neurotransmitters/enzymes ————————————»

    Brain dysfunction————————————————»

    Verbal IQ/cognition ———————————————»

    Hormones ————————————————————»

        Drug use/abuse ————————————————»

        Peer influences————————————————»

        Mental illness ————————————————»

        Strain ————————————————————»

        Destructive labeling————————————————»

        Employment problems ———————————»

        Relationship problems————————————————»

Preventing crime, according to Robinson, will require the implementation of proactive strategies designed to improve early-life experiences, to channel childhood and adolescent development and allow and encourage individuals to develop to their fullest potential; to increase adaptive behaviors; and to minimize the development of maladaptive, aggressive, and antisocial behaviors. However, Robinson never explains how these strategies might be implemented.

Robinson blames the continuing crime problem on the unrelenting pursuit of a crime-control model based on criminal justice, and attributes this pursuit to two factors: first, the adoption of laws by politicians that have eroded constitutional protections and made it easier for the police, the courts, and corrections to investigate, arrest, detain, convict and punish; and second, to media coverage that generates fear in the public, making it more likely for citizens to support tougher crime-fighting methods, even at the expense of their own freedoms. "Myths and stereotypes about crime, criminals, and criminal justice," says Robinson "are created when acts are defined as crimes by the criminal law. These myths and stereotypes are reinforced as the mass media broadcast stories about crime, criminals, and criminal justice. Myths and stereotypes are also reinforced as the police, courts, and corrections enforce the criminal law. The massive criminal justice expansion of the last thirty years of the twentieth century [is] an expansion driven not by facts about crime or increasing crime rates but by politics, fear, and the desire to be punitive—

and at times downright hateful—toward certain segments of the population" (Robinson 2002, preface).

Ironically, Robinson's theory is also a product of myth. A myth is by definition, "an unfounded or false notion." Robinson's assertion that the risk factors selected by him are "validated by scientific evidence" is an unfounded and false notion. Scientific evidence to validate each of the risk factors he identifies does not exist.

Political scientists William Lyons and Stuart Scheingold are convinced that the causes of crime lie in an array of social, economic, and cultural factors, which politicians campaigning against crime use to divert the public's attention away from underlying social, economic, and cultural problems. In other words, politicians use victimization and the fear of crime to win and hold public office. Lyon's and Scheingold's assertion is that a fixation with punishment, along with a tendency on the part of political leaders to ignore crime prevention and instead bombard the public with myths, misconceptions, and half-truths, has resulted in a confused citizenry and the perpetuation of ineffective approaches to solving the crime problem.

Public ignorance, the media's infatuation with sensationalism, and misrepresentations articulated by politicians may all inhibit progress toward discovering what causes criminal behavior and how to prevent it. But it is the ideological and intellectual competition between scholars, who cannot agree among themselves about what causes criminal behavior that creates conditions ideal for the formation of an environment, which breeds ignorance and allows sensationalism and misrepresentation to thrive. If the community of scholars engaged in criminal-justice research want the public and governing bodies to listen to what they have to say about criminal behavior; if they want policies and practices adopted that are based on their findings; and if they want the media to be more objective and less sensational in their reporting about crime, they will have to offer more than just correlative evidence as proof to support their findings.

"Correlation" is a mathematical term used to reflect the relationship between two different variables. The correlation can be positive, negative, or zero. A positive correlation indicates that as one variable increases, the other variable tends to increase. Conversely, a negative correlation indicates that as one variable decreases, the other variable tends to decrease. A zero correlation indicates there is no relationship between the variables. Contrary to popular belief, however, just because there is a mathematical correlation between two variables does not mean there is a causal relationship between the two variables. A correlation may provide a direction for further investigation, but it does not reveal a cause. For example, just because there is a high correlation between the incidence of psychological trauma and criminal behavior does not mean that psychological trauma causes criminal behavior. The same can be said about the correlation between crime and sociological factors, biological factors, and socio-biological factors. A high correlation between poor socio-economic conditions and criminal behavior does not mean that poor socio-economic conditions cause criminal behavior any more than a high correlation between substance abuse and criminal behavior means that substance abuse causes criminal behavior.

> The invalid assumption that correlation implies cause is probably among the two or three most serious and common errors of human reasoning. (Gould 1981, p.242)

Inferring that a high correlation (either negative or positive) between two factors establishes a causal relationship between the two factors is erroneous. Unfortunately, all of the research conducted to date into what causes criminal behavior has revealed nothing more than correlative evidence and very few of the researchers—particularly very few of the social science researchers—acknowledge this fact. Researchers searching for a biological etiology are generally more forthright in declaring their results correlative and cautioning others not to draw any conclusions from the data. It is the use of correlative evidence that sustains the argument between the classical and positivist schools over what causes criminal behavior and how to prevent it, which only serves to perpetuate myths, intuitive beliefs, and mistaken ideas. If the field of criminology hopes to mature to the level of a true discipline or science, it must reconcile its diversity of thought. There must be what Edward O. Wilson refers to as "consilience," or unity of knowledge. Wilson says:

> Most of the issues that vex humanity daily (ethnic conflict, arms escalation, overpopulation, abortion, environment, endemic poverty, [and crime]) … cannot be solved without integrating knowledge from the natural sciences with that of the social sciences and humanities.

> The crucial difference between [medical science and social science] is consilience. The medical sciences have it and the social sciences do not.

Medical scientists build upon a coherent foundation of molecular and cell biology. They pursue elements of health and illness all the way down to the level of biophysical chemistry. The success of their individual projects depends on the fidelity of their experimental design to fundamental principles, which the researchers endeavor to make consistent across all levels of biological organization from the whole organism down, step by step, to the molecule.

In contrast, ... the efforts of social scientists are snarled by disunity and a failure of vision. The reason for the confusion is ... because social scientists spurn the idea of the hierarchical ordering of knowledge that unites and drives the natural sciences. Split into independent cadres [social scientists] ... seldom speak the same technical language from one specialty to the next. (Wilson 1999, p.13 and p. 198)

Some—perhaps many—social scientists might take issue with Wilson over whether or not medical science is as pure and harmonious as Wilson depicts it. The ongoing dispute between medical scientists over whether chemical imbalance in the brain is a valid concept, for example, is an indication that not all is well among the descendants of Hippocrates and Galen. There should be no disagreement, however, over whether there is a need to unify the knowledge developed by the various schools of thought about what causes criminal behavior and how it can be prevented.

The choice seems simple: to either set aside parochial differences, stop promoting intuition based ideas as scientific findings and engage in a joint effort to construct an approach to crime prevention based on rational thought, careful planning, objective data, and reasonable expectations: or continue building another Winchester Mystery House, filled with dead-end hallways, meaningless stairways, and doorways to nowhere. If the current approach to solving the problem does not change, the general public, politicians, and others who scrutinize and evaluate crime prevention programs should adjust their expectations, because they will always be disappointed and dissatisfied with the results produced by the existing approach.

Part 4

Addendum

DNA (Deoxyribonucleic Acid) Analysis

There has been one development in recent years involving the relationship between biology and crime that has not solved the mystery of what causes criminal behavior or how to prevent it, but has made for remarkable improvements in the process of determining whether a person accused of a crime is guilty or not guilty. That development involves the analysis of deoxyribonucleic acid, or DNA, which is a chemical present in most living things that determines all inborn human traits (Lazer 2004).

Every part of the body is made up of multiple cells. Each cell contains the same DNA, which is composed of four other chemicals called building blocks or bases. Each chemical has a scientific name that is as complicated as that of DNA itself. For the sake of simplicity, these four DNA building blocks are commonly referred to by the letters A (Adenine), T (Thymine), G (Guanine), and C (Cytosine). The sequence of the base chemicals present in each strand of DNA provides a genetic code that is transmitted from one generation to another through the male sperm and female egg. Using a highly complex process, forensic scientists can compare the genetic code from a

DNA sample left at a crime scene—such as hair, saliva, blood, skin, or semen—to the genetic code of a DNA sample taken from a suspect, and thereby determine whether the two samples come from the same individual.

In 1996, the federal government released a report entitled *Convicted by Juries, Exonerated by Science,* in which it was revealed that since the 1980s, when DNA testing was first introduced in the United States, 110 convicted and sentenced felons, twelve of whom had been on death row, had been released after DNA testing had established that they had not been the perpetrator of the crime for which they had been convicted. The average time served for all those exonerated was seven years. One of the twelve prisoners sentenced to death had served seventeen years awaiting execution. (Conners et al. 1996).

On the opposite side of the justice ledger—the victims' side—DNA analysis is being used to solve crimes that might otherwise go unsolved and the perpetrators unpunished. DNA samples are collected from convicted felons, and are kept available for retrieval and comparison purposes. There is no national report documenting the number of cases solved through this process. However, according to the Federal Bureau of Investigation, as of December 1999, six hundred DNA samples maintained in their database—known as CODIS, or the Combined DNA Index

System—have matched DNA samples collected during investigations of more than 1100 previously unsolved crimes. In a more recent case, a man was convicted in New York State in November 2005 for a knifepoint rape he had committed thirty-two years earlier, after analysis of DNA samples collected at the crime scene indicated that they were identical to his. Such analysis had not been possible at the time the crime was committed (FBI 2000).

Brain Fingerprinting

"Brain fingerprinting" is a technique developed by Larry Farwell, PhD, former Harvard University research associate and founder of the Brain Wave Institute, now headquartered in Seattle, Washington (Farwell and Smith 2001). The technique is based on the theory that a complete history of every human being's thoughts and activities—including any criminal thoughts or activities—are stored within the brain. Using an electroencephalograph (EEG) machine connected to a sensor-studded headband worn by the suspect, the suspect is presented with a series of words and pictures flashed on a video monitor. Some of the words and pictures are by design relevant to the crime in question, and some are totally irrelevant. Unlike in a polygraph test, no questions are posed to the suspect.

Farwell claims that if the suspect's brain contains a memory of the crime in question, the brain will transmit an electrical impulse in response to the relevant words or pictures, but will be unresponsive to irrelevant words or pictures. Conversely, if the suspect's brain contains no memory of the crime in question, the brain will be unresponsive to both relevant and irrelevant words and pictures. The entire process is controlled by computer, including the presentation of the memory stimuli, the recording of the brain activity, and the statistical analysis of the responses, which is assisted by a mathematical data-analysis algorithm. The results of brain fingerprinting have been admitted as evidence in appeals to convictions in at least two different cases in two different states.

Case Number 1: *Terry J. Harrington v. the State of Iowa*

In February 2003, the Iowa State Supreme Court reversed the twenty-four-year-old murder conviction of Terry Harrington, based on the results of a brain finger-printing test. The report presented to the court stated that the electrical responses from Harrington's brain, which were stimulated by words and pictures about the crime, indicated that Harrington had no memory of the murder stored in his brain. The electrical responses did reflect, however, that the memories stored in his brain *did* support his alibi. The court ordered that Harrington be retried or released. In October 2003, the State of Iowa elected not to retry Harrington, and he was released.

Case Number 2: *Jimmie Ray Slaughter v. the State of Okalahoma*

In March 2005, Slaughter was executed for the 1991 murder of a twenty-nine-year-old woman and her eleven-month-old daughter, despite the results of a brain fingerprinting analysis presented on appeal to the Oklahoma Pardon and Parole Board that indicated that Slaughter had no memories stored in his brain that would indicate that he had committed the crime.

META-ANALYSIS

A meta-analysis is a set of statistical techniques used to combine the results from different studies about the same question to derive an overall estimate of results for the combination of studies. Consistent with what seems to be a theme among those trying to solve the mystery of criminal behavior, not everyone has confidence in this technique:

> My objections to meta-analysis are purely pragmatic. It does not work nearly as well as we might want it to work. The problems are so deep and so numerous that the results are simply not reliable. The work of LeLorier et al. adds to the evidence that meta-analysis simply does not work very well in practice.
>
> As it is practiced and as it is reported in our leading journals, meta-analysis is often deeply flawed. Many people cite high-sounding guidelines, and I am sure that all truly want to do a superior analysis, but meta-analysis often fails in ways that seem to be invisible to the analyst.
>
> The advocates of meta-analysis and evidence-based medicine should undertake research that

might demonstrate that meta-analyses in the real world—not just in theory—improve health outcomes in patients. Review of the long history of randomized, controlled trials, individually weak for this specific purpose, has led to overwhelming evidence of efficacy. I am not willing to abandon that history to join those now promoting meta-analysis as the answer, no matter how pretty the underlying theory, until its defects are honestly exposed and corrected. The knowledgeable, thoughtful, traditional review of the original literature remains the closest thing we have to a gold standard for summarizing disparate evidence in medicine.

(Excerpts from a letter sent by John C. Blailar II, professor emeritus in the department of health studies at the University of Chicago to the New England Journal of Medicine (NEJM) in response to letters published by the NEJM regarding LeLorier et al. 1997, "Discrepancies Between Meta-Analyses and Subsequent Large Randomized, Controlled Trials," NEJM, 337, 536–542 and Blailar's accompanying editorial, 559–561, reprinted in The Little Handbook of Statistical Practices (2001).

Gerard E. Dallal, chief of the biostatistics unit of the Human Nutrition Research Center at Tufts University says that there are three problems with meta-analysis: (1) publication bias; (2) variation in the quality of studies; and (3) absence of large-scale, high quality studies.

1. Publication bias (sometimes called the file-drawer problem), says Dallal, occurs because the meta-analysis is applied only to studies that have been published, which are more likely to report an effect than non-published studies. Studies showing no effect are more likely to have been filed away in a drawer and not published.

2. Variation in the quality of studies negatively impacts the validity of meta-analysis because the results of poorly designed studies are given the same weight as those of well designed studies.

3. Because large-scale, high-quality trials are scarce, publication bias and variation in the quality of those studies that are available make it impossible to draw any clear conclusions.

Readers who may be interested can learn more about this debatable technique by reading the following. Works supporting meta-analysis include: *The Handbook of Research Statistics* (Cooper and Hedges 1994); *Statistical*

Methods of Meta-Analysis (Hedges and Olkin 1985); and Meta-Analysis: Cumulating Research Findings Across Studies (Hunter, Schmidt, and Jackson, 1982). Works criticizing meta-analysis include: *An Abuse of Research Integration* (Eysenck 1984); *Meta-Analysis: Sense or Nonsense* (Eysenck 1992); and *Meta-analysis: Statistical Alchemy for the 21st Century* (Liberati 1995).

INTERNATIONAL APPROACHES TO CRIME PREVENTION

In 1995, the Castine Research Corporation conducted a study, funded by the crime and prevention unit of the police department of the British Home Office. The results of the Castine study, *Building A Safer Society: Strategic Approaches to Crime Prevention* were published by the University of Chicago Press in Volume 19 *of Crime and Justice: A Review of Research*, which is one of a series of volumes of commissioned essays on crime-related topics (Tonry and Petersila 1999).

Although the Castine study and the University of Maryland study had similar objectives (both sought to identify crime prevention programs that work), there are at least two major differences between the two studies.

The first difference is that the Castine study gave more consideration to studies completed in countries other than the United States, perhaps because the source of the funds used to underwrite the study was the United Kingdom, or because, according to the editors of the study, "Crime prevention strategies, program development, and research have received more sustained attention in Western Europe than in North America."

The second difference is in the methods used to complete the two studies. The Castine study did not employ any standardized rating instrument or system to evaluate the strategies it reviewed. Instead, the Castine group arbitrarily established four categorical areas of interest: 1) Law Enforcement and Criminal Justice Prevention; 2) Community Crime Prevention; 3) Developmental Crime Prevention; and 4) Situational Crime Prevention.

Law Enforcement and Criminal Justice Prevention

Law enforcement and criminal justice strategies are strategies which are seen as operating directly through deterrence, incapacitation, and rehabilitation; and indirectly through their effects on socialization, such as those engendered by prisons.

Community Crime Prevention

Community crime prevention strategies are strategies that are intended to change the social conditions that are believed to sustain crime in residential communities—actions such as community organizing, tenant involvement, resource mobilization, community defense, preserving order, and protecting the vulnerable.

Developmental Crime Prevention

Developmental crime prevention strategies are strategies which are predicated on the belief that criminal behavior is determined by behavioral and attitudinal patterns that have been learned during an individual's development. A parenting training program designed to improve parenting skills of at-risk youth is one example of a developmental crime prevention strategy.

Situational Crime Prevention

Situational crime prevention strategies are strategies that seek to reduce opportunities for specific categories of crime by increasing the associated risks and difficulties, and by reducing the rewards. Target-hardening, which involves the installation of physical barriers, is one of the most common situational crime prevention methods.

After establishing these categories of interest, writers were commissioned to prepare essays on three of the four major categories. No essays were solicited or commissioned on law enforcement and criminal justice prevention because according to the editors there is an emerging consensus among researchers and public officials in many countries that law enforcement's effects are limited and modest, and that public safety policies that rely solely or primarily on law enforcement are incomplete and insufficiently protect the public. Criminal sanctions are increasingly understood, claim the editors, to have only modest effects on crime rates or patterns. Prison and jail sentences in many cases, they say, further harm already-damaged people, and increase the likelihood that a criminal will re-offend. Each essay was based on the author's review of published results of studies conducted by other researchers. Drafts of each writer's essay were then presented to a conference of scholars who offered suggestions for change. In addition, each draft was critiqued by crime and justice editors, as well as by anonymous referees, after which each writer prepared a final version of the essay for publication.

The United States' alleged preoccupation with criminal-justice prevention remedies is attributed by the editors to elected officials who share the belief that crime represents a moral failure on the part of the wrongdoer, and that law enforcement, including the imposition of sanctions that stress the condemnation of the offender, is the only morally appropriate, broad-based state policy for crime prevention. Western European countries, in contrast to the United States, are credited with investing more resources in implementing community developmental and situational prevention initiatives. France, England, Sweden, and the Netherlands have established specialized governmental agencies to develop, test, and evaluate crime prevention programs—agencies which utilize non-law-enforcement techniques.

The results of the International Crime Victim Survey suggest that the Castine group's assertion that crime prevention in the United States is less effective than crime prevention in Western Europe may not be valid. The International Crime Victim Survey (ICVS) is a standardized tool used to collect information about the prevalence of crime directly from households in: Australia, Belgium, Canada, Spain, Denmark, England, Wales, Finland, France, Japan, the Netherlands, Northern Ireland, Poland, Portugal, Scotland, Sweden, Switzerland, the United States, Albania, Argentina, Azerbaijan, Belarus, Botswana, Bulgaria, Cambodia, Colombia, Croatia, the Czech Republic, Estonia, Georgia, Hungary, Latvia, Lesotho, Lithuania, Mongolia, Mozambique, Namibia, Nigeria, Panama, the Philippines, Poland, South Korea, Romania, Russia, Slovenia, South Africa, Swaziland, Uganda, Ukraine, and Zambia (Alvazzi et al. 2003). Coordinated by the Netherlands Department of Justice in conjunction with the United Nations Interregional Crime and Justice Institute, the ICVS has been conducted four times since 1989, the most recent survey having occurred in 2000.

The results of this last survey indicate that when asked whether they had been the victim of one or more crimes in the preceding year, 24 percent of the households surveyed in Australia, England and Wales, the Netherlands, and Sweden responded in the affirmative. In contrast, between 20 and 24 percent of the households surveyed in Canada, Scotland, Denmark, Poland, Belgium, France, and the United States reported that they had been victimized. In Finland, Spain, Switzerland, Portugal, Japan, and Northern Ireland, less than 20 percent of the households surveyed reported that they had been victimized in the previous year.

In terms of specific crimes, the results of the 2000 survey indicated that:

- The risk of having been a victim of car theft was 2.6 percent in England, 2.1 percent in Wales, 2.1 percent in Australia, 1.9 percent in France, and 0.5 percent or less in Japan, Switzerland, Spain, the United States, Finland and the Netherlands. The risk of having been a victim of burglary or attempted burglary was 7 percent in Australia, 5 percent in England and Wales, and 4 percent in Canada, Denmark, and Belgium.

- The risk of having been a victim of robbery, assault with force, or sexual assault over 3 percent in Australia, England, Wales, Canada, Scotland, and

Finland, and less than 2 percent in the United States, Belgium, Spain, Portugal, and Japan.

• Women in Sweden, Finland, Australia, England, and Wales had the highest risk of having been sexually assaulted, and women in Japan, Northern Ireland, Poland, and Portugal had the lowest risk.

Contrary to what the Castine group asserted, the International Crime Victim Survey data suggests that the crime prevention programs being promoted by Western European countries are no more successful than those used in the United States; and may in some cases be less successful.

Sentencing Guidelines

Sentencing guidelines and mandatory minimum prison sentences have been a point of consternation to the federal judiciary since 1987, when the United States Sentencing Commission (USSC)—created by Congress with the passage of the Sentencing Reform Act of 1984—promulgated guidelines for use by judges when sentencing a criminal convicted of violating a federal law, which imposed severe restraints on judicial discretion. Many state legislatures, much to the chagrin of state-level judges, passed similar legislation, which led to the formulation of a variety of sentencing guidelines modeled after the federal guidelines (Hofer et al. 2004).

Prior to the passage of the Sentencing Reform Act and the creation of the Sentencing Commission, penalties for federal crimes were broadly defined and judges were allowed to impose, without explanation or justification, whatever penalty they felt was appropriate. This sentencing process produced wide variations in sentences imposed even within the same judicial jurisdiction. One offender might have been given probation, while another offender, with the same criminal history, convicted of the same crime, would be sent to prison. The outcome was left to judicial discretion. The intent of sentencing guidelines was to reduce disparity in the sentencing process, and to promote fairness, equity, consistency and certainty in sentencing by requiring judges to justify their sentences in accordance with established guidelines. This manifestly restricted judicial discretion. After the imposition of sentencing guidelines, criminals convicted of the same a particular crime, with like criminal histories could expect to receive the same sentence.

Follow-up studies designed to assess the effectiveness of sentencing guidelines have indicated that these guidelines have been generally successful. Sentencing is more transparent, based on articulated reasons stated in open court and reviewable on appeal. Punishment is more certain and predictable, allowing the parties to better anticipate the sentencing consequences of case facts, and allowing the system to better predict the impact of changes in policy on prison populations and correctional resources. Sentence severity has been increased for many types of crime, in some cases substantially. Most important, the guidelines do not admit consideration of factors, such as race or ethnicity that are irrelevant to the purpose of sentencing. There is less inter-judge disparity for similar offenders committing similar offenses. (Hofer et al. p.xvi)

The judicial lament about sentencing guidelines was that the corresponding loss of judicial discretion has resulted in too many people being incarcerated for far too long, at a time when revenue is scarce and needs to be prudently spent (Kennedy 2003). The data do conclusively show that since the advent of sentencing guidelines, the number of criminals sentenced to prison has increased by nearly 20 percent, and that the use of probation, without confinement as a condition, has decreased nearly 50 percent (Stith and Cubranes 1998). However, the judiciary offers no support for its argument, other than its intuitive beliefs based on experience, that the increased use of incarceration and the decreased use of probation are proof that too many people are being incarcerated, that criminal justice resources are being misspent, or that punishments are too severe and sentences are too long.

According to the ABA, the role of a judge in a criminal trial is like that of an umpire during a baseball game. The judge is not on either side; the judge is neutral. The judge's job in a criminal trial is to preside over the process and ensure that the proceedings are conducted in accordance with the law and with pre-established rules that have been designed to ensure that the proceedings are fair and impartial. Judicial discretion is purposely limited to deciding questions of law and rule.

Given the rigid structure that surrounds the trial process and the limits imposed on judicial discretion, it is hard to understand why there is any debate over whether the sentencing process in a criminal trial should be structured or whether the sentence imposed should be left to the unfettered discretion of a judge. If rules and laws are considered essential to guarantee fairness and impartiality in criminal trial proceedings, why should guidelines not be used to ensure uniformity and equity in sentencing?

Judicial objection to sentencing guidelines appears to be less about concern for the appropriate use of finite financial resources and the overuse of prison as a sanction than about regaining the power, control, and influence that judges enjoyed prior to the introduction of sentencing guidelines.

In January 2005, the Supreme Court of the United States (in *United States v. Booker*) declared that the mandatory application of federal sentencing guidelines were unconstitutional because they required judges to consider factors when sentencing that had not been considered by the jury or proven during the trial. The Court said this practice violates the Sixth Amendment of the Constitution, which guarantees a defendant the right to a jury trial, because the factors considered by the judge were not being heard by the jury. The Court allowed that judges could consult the guidelines in determining reasonable sentences, but only on an advisory basis—which is confusing even to some legal scholars, who are unable to explain why the Court would instruct judges to consult guidelines, even as merely advisory tools, that have been declared unconstitutional.

It is far too early to determine the eventual outcome of this ruling. The United States Congress can try to amend the governing legislation that authorizes the federal sentencing guidelines; the Sentencing Commission can try to overcome the Court's objections administratively by revising the federal guidelines; or the federal government and the affected states may adopt a different system, such as the two-tier system used by Kansas, which provides for a separate sentencing phase during which the jury, not the judge, identifies the factors that can be used to determine the length of a prison sentence (USSC 2006).

Unless some action is taken that mandates judges must continue to use sentencing guidelines, judges have regained their power of discretion, and the criminal justice system may not be the better for it. Justice Sandra Day O'Connor, in dissent to the high Court's decision, warned that over twenty years of sentencing reform will be all but lost, and that tens of thousands of criminal judgments will be in jeopardy.

CRIME RATES AND RECIDIVISM RATES

The two most commonly used means for measuring the effectiveness of crime prevention programs are crime rates and recidivism rates. Both forms of measurement are of questionable value (DiIulio 1993).

Crime Rates

Crime rates, birth rates, divorce rates, unemployment rates, and school drop-out rates are all gross indicators of how often a general activity or event occurs. The rate at which a particular activity or event occurs does not measure performance or explain why there are increases or decreases in a particular activity or event. Determining why the rate of a particular activity or event increases or decreases requires investigators to identify and analyze all of the factors that cause the activity or event to occur. For example, to determine why birth rates increase or decrease, analysts not only consider the effects of birth-control methods, they also factor in the impact of abortion and the influence of abstinence. Several factors—such as population density, degree of urbanization, variations in population composition, population stability, modes of transportation, economic conditions, family cohesiveness, cultural activities, climate, law enforcement strength, investigative emphasis, and crime-reporting practices—have been identified that appear to affect the volume and type of crime that occurs in a given place, but there is only one factor that is known to influence the volume of crime, and that is the number of people in the prime prone age group that help comprise the total population. There is no dispute over the fact that most crime is committed by white males between the ages of fifteen and twenty-nine. It is known for certain that when the number of white males in this age group rises, crime rates rise as well. Conversely, crime rates definitely go down when the number of white males in this cohort declines (FBI 2005).

In the 2005 edition of *Crime in the United States*, the United States Department of Justice criticizes the news media, tourism agencies, and other groups with an interest in crime in the United States for using factors such as crime rates to create misleading perceptions that adversely affect certain cities and counties. The Department of Justice does not state who or what the "other groups" with an interest in crime are, but it should certainly include the multitude of philosophers, scholars, intellectuals from various disciplines, students, practitioners, judges, prosecuting attorneys, defense lawyers, ex-offenders, victims, police officers, private citizen advisory groups, individual concerned citizens, and political leaders who have used crime rates without analysis to support and promote a particular approach to solving the crime problem. Classical-school thinkers—those who argue that criminal behavior is a willful activity, committed voluntarily—attribute increases in crime rates to being soft on crime and failing to punish criminal offenders properly. Positivist thinkers—those who argue that criminal behavior is an involuntary activity caused by psychological trauma, social circumstances, biological factors or some other catalytic agent—blame crime-rate increases on the failure to treat criminal offenders and ameliorate the conditions that breed criminals. Crime rates offer no insight into what causes criminal behavior or how to prevent it, and they provide no clue as to the effectiveness of any particular crime prevention program.

Recidivism Rates

Recidivism rates are used to measure how many criminals re-offend after release from prison, probation, parole, or any other corrections program. Recidivism rates are not a reliable or effective indicator for measuring the success or failure of crime prevention programs for at least two reasons. First, there is no uniform standard that specifies how much time should elapse after an offender is released from a crime prevention program before the offender should be considered a non-recidivist. Second, there is no consensus on what events should signify failure (Beck 2001; Carcach 1999).

There is no mandatory requirement for states or the federal government to monitor or report information on what happens to an offender after being released from prison or from a specific program (such as one designed to treat sex offenders or substance abusers). And even if such a requirement existed, there is no system in place to track an offender after release or to process the information. The time frame for a study, or the length of time an offender or group of offenders is monitored in any given recidivism study is arbitrarily established. The time-frame for some studies is between three and five years; but many studies are limited to a much shorter period of time—90 to 180 days. An offender is only considered a recidivist if he or she fails within the time frame established for a particular study. If the offender re-offends after this time period has elapsed, he or she is not counted as a recidivist.

Like the time-frame for recidivism studies, the events used to signify failure in a given recidivism study often vary as well. Some studies consider an offender a failure if he or she is *arrested* within the study's established time frame. Other studies use *reconviction* as the standard for signifying failure. Still others use *return to prison* as the triggering event. No study has ever been conducted that follows an offender or group of offenders for the remainder of their lives after release from prison, parole, or probation.

Absent a uniform time-frame and consensus regarding what constitutes failure, recidivism rates are nothing more than artificial numbers that, like crime rates, offer no real insight into what causes criminal behavior or how to prevent it; and they provide no clue as to the effectiveness of any particular crime prevention program.

About the Author

The author holds a BA in psychology from Willamette University (1964), an MS in community service and public affairs from the University of Oregon (1974), and a PhD in educational policy and management from the University of Oregon (1995). He was employed for thirty years—for twenty years at the executive level—administering state government corrections programs and institutions for adult criminals, juvenile delinquents, and the criminally insane. He has been an adjunct faculty member in the Department of Criminal Justice at Western Oregon University, and an instructor at the National Academy for Corrections. He is currently working as a security consultant.

Bibliography

Ackoff, R. L. *The Art of Problem Solving*. New York: John Wiley & Sons, Inc., 1987.

Advisory Committee on Student Financial Assistance (2002) *Empty Promises: The Myth of College Access in America*.
Online: http://www.ed.gov/offices/AC/ACSFA/ emptypromises.pdf

Agnew, R. K., *Pressured Into Crime: An Overview of Strain Theory*. Los Angles, CA: Roxbury Publishing, 2006.

Aguayo, T. (May 19, 2006). "Youth who killed at 12 gets 30 years for violating probation," *New York Times*.

Alcock, J. *The Triumph of Sociobiology*. New York, NY: Oxford University Press, 2003.

Alcock, J. (7th ed.) *Animal Behavior: An Evolutionary Approach*. Sunderland, CT: Sinauer Associates, Inc., 2001.

Alexander, J. C., Boudon, R. and Cherkaoui, M. (eds.) *The Classical Tradition in Sociology: The American Tradition*. London: Sage Publications, 1997.

Alexander, J. C. and Smith, P. *The Cambridge Companion to Durkheim*. New York, NY: Cambridge University Press, 2005.

Alexander, M. (November 1999). "Sexual offender treatment efficacy revisited." *Sexual Abuse: A Journal of Research and Treatment,* 11 (2), 101–116.

Alvazzi, A., VanDijk, J. M., Van Kesteren, J., and Mayhew, P., IVCS (2003) International Working Group. *International Victims Survey (IVCS), 1989–2000.* Interregional Crime and Justice Research Institute (UNICRI [Producers]), for Political and Social Research (Distributors).

American Bar Association, Justice Kennedy Commission. (June 23, 2004) "Report to the house of delegates." Online: http://www.abanet.org/crimijust/kennedy

American Correctional Association. "Standards & accreditation." Online: http://www.aca.org.standards

American Psychiatric Association. *Diagnostic and Statistical Manual of Mental Disorders.* (4th ed.), Washington DC: American Psychiatric Association, 2000.

Anderson, D. A. "The Aggregate Burden of Crime" (October 1999). *The Journal of Law and Economics*, 42 (2) 611–642.

Anderson, J. R. *Cognitive Psychology and its Implications.* (5th ed.), New York, NY: Worth Publishing, 1995.

Arraj, J. and Arraj, T. *William Sheldon: A Forgotten Giant of American Psychology.* Chiloquin, OR: Inner Growth Books, 1994.

Ashton, C. H. *Chemical Imbalance*, Newcastle: School of Neurosciences, Division of Psychiatry: 2001.

Associated Press (November 10, 2005). "DNA leads to conviction after 32 years,"
Online: http://cnn.worldnews.com

Avshalom, C., McClay, J., Moffitt, T. E., Mill, J., Martin, J., Craig, I. W., Taylor, A. and Poulton, R. (August 2002). "Role of Genotype in Cycle of Violence in Maltreated Children." *Science* 2 851–854.

Bauer, L. and Owens, S. D. (May 2004). *Justice Expenditures and Employment in the United States, 2001.* Washington DC: U.S. Department of Justice.

Beardsley, M. C. (ed.). *European Philosophers from Descartes to Nietzsche.* Toronto: Random House, 1988.

Beck, A. R. (May 2001). *Recidivism: A Fruit-Salad Concept in the Criminal Justice System.*
Online: http://www.justiceconcepts.com/recidivism

Becker, G. S. *The Economic Approach to Human Behavior.* Chicago: University of Chicago Press, 1976.

Becker, H. *Outsiders: Studies in the Sociology of Deviance.* NY: Free Press, 1963.

Beckett, K. *Making Crime Pay: Law and Order in Contemporary American Politics.* New York, NY: Oxford University Press, 1997.

Bedau, H. A. *The Death Penalty in America.* New York, NY: Oxford University Press, 1982.

Bedau, H. and Cassel, P. (eds.) *Debating the Death Penalty: Should America Have Capital Punishment?* New York, NY: Oxford University Press, 2004.

Bentham, J. *An Introduction to the Principles of Morals and Legislation.* New York, NY: Oxford University Press, 1996.

Berk, R. *New Claims About Executions and General Deterrence: Déjà Vu All Over Again.* (July 19, 2004) Online: http://www.stat.ucla.edu

Berlin, I. (ed.). *The Age of Enlightenment: the 18th Century Philosophers.* Boston: Houghton Mifflin, 1956

Bonczar, T. P. and Snell, T. L. *Capital Punishment 2004.* (November 2005). Washington DC: Department of Justice.

Browning, G., Halcli, A., Hewlett, N., and Webster, F. (eds.) *Understanding Contemporary Society: Theories of the Present.* London: Sage, 1999.

Braithwaite, J. *Crime, Shame and Reintegration.* London: Cambridge University Press, 1989.

Breggin, P. R. and Cohen, D. *Your Drug May Be Your Problem: How and Why to Stop Taking Psychiatric Medications.* Reading, MA: Perseus Books, 1999.

Bufkin, J. L. and Luttrell, V. R., (2005) "Neuroimaging studies of aggressive and violent behavior: current implications for criminology and criminal justice" in *Trauma, Violence & Abuse,* 6 (2) 176–191.

Bureau of Labor Statistics, *Unemployment Rates*, (May 2006) Washington DC: U. S. Department of Labor. Online: http://www.data.bls.gov

Bureau of Labor Statistics, "Labor force statistics from the current population survey-1994-2004." (2005) Washington DC: U.S. Department of Labor. Online: http://www.data.bls.gov

Buss, D. M. *Evolutionary Psychology: the New Science of the Mind.* Boston: Allyn and Bacon, 1999.

Caixeta, M. (Summer 1996). "A Critical Look at Current Concepts of Personality Disorders: Moral v. Medical Aspects." *International Journal of Psychopathology, Psychopharmacology, and Psychotherapy* (IJPPP), Vol. 1, No. 1. Online: http://www.psycom.net

Callan, P. M. (September 2004) *Measuring Up 2004: the National Report Card on Higher Education.* Washington DC: The National Center for Public Policy and Higher Education

Campling, P. and Haigh, R. (eds.) *Therapeutic Communities: Past, Present and Future.* London: Jessica Kingsley Publishers, 1999.

Carcach, S. L. *Recidivism Among Juvenile Offenders: An Analysis of Times to Reappearance in Court.* (1999) Australia: Court Research and Public Policy.

Carver, J. M. (2002). "The Chemical Imbalance in Mental Health Problems." Portsmouth: Joseph M. Carver, PhD, Inc.
Online: http://www.mental-health-matters.com/articles

Catalano, S. H. (December 2004). *Criminal Victimization in the United States, 2002,* Washington DC: U. S. Department of Justice.

Cassell, P. G. (2004) "In Defense of the Death Penalty," in H. Bedau and P. Cassel (eds.), *Debating the death penalty: should America have capital punishment?* New York: Oxford University Press.

Center for Sex Offender Management (May 2001) "Recidivism of Sex Offenders," Washington DC: Department of Justice.
Online: http://www.csom.org./pubs/recidsexof.pdf

Clarke, R. G. and Mayhew, P. (eds.) (1980). "Designing out crime." Home Office and Research Planning Unit.
Online: http://www.aic.gov.au/publications/crimeprev/part3

Classen, R. *Restorative Justice—Fundamental Principles*. (1995). Center for Peacemaking and Conflict Studies, Fresno Pacific University.

Cloward, R. and Ohlin, L. *Opportunity Delinquency*. New York, NY: Free Press, 1960.

Clubb, L. G. *Della Porta's Life*. Princeton, NJ: Princeton University Press, 1965.

Cohen, A. *Delinquent Boys*. Glencoe, Ill: Free Press, 1955.

Cohen, R. L. (August 1995). "Probation and Parole Violators in State Prison, 1991." Washington DC: Bureau of Justice Statistics

College Board. (October 2005) *Trends in College Pricing*. Online: http://www.collegeboard.com/press/cost05

Conners, E., Lundregan, T. Miller, N. and McEwen, T. (June 1996). *Convicted By Juries, Exonerated By Science: Case Studies in the Use of DNA Evidence to Establish Innocence After Trial*. Washington DC: U. S. Department of Justice, National Institute of Justice.

Cooper, H. M., and Hedges, L. V. (eds.) *The Handbook of Research Synthesis*. New York, NY: Sage, 1994.

Corey, Gerald (4th ed.). *Theory and Practice of Counseling and Psychotherapy.* Pacific Grove, CA: Brooks/Cole Publishing Company, 1991.

Coyne, J. A. *Speciation.* Sunderland, MA: Sinauer Associated, 2004.

Cosmides, L. and Tooby, J. *The Psychological Foundations of Culture in the Adapted Mind,* Barkow, J. H., Cosmides, L. and Tooby, J. (eds.) New York: Oxford University Press, 1992.

Crawford, A. and Gooley, J. (eds.) *Integrating a Victim Perspective Within Criminal Justice*: International Debates. Brookfield, VT: Ashgate, 2000.

Crawford, C. B., and Krebs, D. L. (eds.) *Handbook of Evolutionary Psychology: Ideas, Issues, and Applications.* Mahwah, NJ: Lawrence Erlbaum, 1998.

Cronin, H. (Reprint ed.). *The Ant and the Peacock: Altruism and Sexual Selection from Darwin to Today.* London: Cambridge University Press, 2003.

Currie, E. *Crime and Punishment in America.* New York, NY: Henry Holt and Company, 1998.

Dallal, G. E. *The Little Handbook of Statistical Practice*, (2001), Tufts University.
Online: http://www.StatisticalPractice.com

Damasio, A. *Descartes' Error—Emotion, Reason, and the Human Brain*. New York: G. P. Putnam's Sons, 1994.

Danks, H. (May 31, 2004). "Judge rejects slave trauma as defense in boy's killing." Portland, OR: The Oregonian

Davey, J. D. *The Politics of Prison Expansion: Winning Elections by Waging War on Crime*. Westport, Connecticut: Praeger, 1998.

Dawkins, R. (2nd ed.). *The Selfish Gene*. New York: Oxford University Press, 1989.

DeNauas-Walt, C., Cleveland, R., and Webster, B. H. Jr. (September 2003) *Income in the United States: 2002*. Washington DC: United States Bureau of the Census

Dennett, D. C. *Darwin's Dangerous Idea: Evolution and its Meanings of Life*. New York: Simon & Schuster, 1995.

DeGruy-Leary, J. *Post-Traumatic Slave Syndrome: America's Legacy of Enduring Injury and Healing*. United Kingdom: Uptone Press, 2005.

Dezhbakhsh, H., Rubin, P. H. and Shepherd, J. M. (2003) "Does Capital Punishment Have a Deterrent Effect? New Evidence From Post-Moratorium Panel Data. *American Law and Economics Review*, 5 (2), 344–376.

De Leon, G. *The Therapeutic Community: Theory, Model and Method.* New York, NY: Springer Publishing Company, 2000.

DiIulio, J. J. Jr., Alpert, G. P., Moore, M. H., Cole, G. F., Petersilia, J. Logan, C. H. and Wilson, J. Q. (October 1993) *Performance Measures for the Criminal Justice System.* Washington DC: Department of Justice

DSQIC Staff, (January 15, 2000). "Brain Development: Foundations for Learning & Behavior." DSQIC Dispatch. Logan, Utah: Head Start Region VIII, Disability Services Quality Improvement Center.

Durose, M. R. and Langan, P. A. (December 2004) *Felony Sentences in State Courts, 2002.* Washington DC: Department of Justice.

Eaton T. Fores Research Center. (2003) "There Are No Chemical Imbalances." Online: http://www.etfrc.com

Ehrlich, I. (June 1975) "The Deterrent Effect of Capital Punishment: A Question of Life and Death. *The American Economic Review*, 65(3) 397–417.

Ehrlich, P. R. *Human Natures: Genes, Cultures and the Human Prospect.* Washington DC: Shearwater Books/Island Press, 2000.

Elster, J. (ed.). *Rational Choice.* Oxford: Basil Blackwell, 1986.

Eysenck, H. J. (3rd ed.). *Crime and Personality.* London and Henley: Routledge & Kegan Paul, 1977.

Eysenck, H. J. (1984) "An Abuse of Research Integration. *Journal of Special Education*, 18: 41–59.

Eysenck, H. J. (1992) "Meta-Analysis: Sense or Nonsense?" *Pharmaceutical Medicine*, 6: 113–119.

Farkas, M. A., and Stichman, A. (2002) "Sex Offender Laws: Can Treatment, Punishment, Incapacitation and Public Safety Be Reconciled?" *Criminal Justice Review*, 27 (2), 256–283.

Farwell, L. W., and Smith, S. S. (2001) "Using Brain MERMER Testing to Detect Knowledge Despite Efforts to Conceal." *Journal of Forensic Sciences* 46 (1) 1–9.

Federal Bureau of Investigation, (April 2000) *The FBI's Combined DNA Index System Program: CODIS, a Federal/State Partnership Fighting Violent Crime.* Washington DC: U. S. Department of Justice.

Federal Bureau of Investigation. (2005) *Uniform Crime Report: Crime in the United States, 2004.* Washington DC: U. S. Department of Justice

Feinstein, A. R. (1995) "Meta-Analysis: Statistical Alchemy for the 21st Century." *Journal of Clinical Epidemiology.* 48 (1) 71–79.

Fogler, H. S. and LeBlanc, S. E. *Creative Approaches to Problem Solving.* Upper Saddle River, NJ: PTR Prentice Hall, 1995.

Fishbein, D. H. *Behavioral Perspectives in Criminology.* Belmont, CA: Wadsworth Publishing, 2000.

Fishbein, D. and Pease, S. (1988). "The Effects of Diet on Behavior: Implications for Criminology and Corrections."

Research in Corrections, Volume 1, Issue 2. Washington DC: Robert J. Kutak Foundation and the National Institute of Correction

Foucault, M. *Discipline and Punish: the Birth of Prison*. New York, NY: Pantheon, 1977.

Friel, C. M., Vaughn, J. B. and del Carmen, R. (1986). *Electronic Monitoring and Correctional Policy: the Technology and its Application*. Washington DC: Department of Justice.

Furby, L., Weinrott, M. R. and Blackshaw, L. (1989) "Sex Offender Recidivism: A Review. *Psychological Bulletin* 105.

Furman v. Georgia 408 U. S. 238

Garland, D. *Punishment and Modern Society*. Chicago: University of Chicago Press, 1990.

Garrison, A. H. (2003). "Terrorism: the Nature of its History." Criminal Justice Studies. 16(1) 39–52.

Gaubatz, K. *Crime in the Public Mind*. Ann Arbor: University of Michigan, 1995.

Geason, S. and Wilson, P. R. *Crime Prevention: Theory and Practice.* Canberra: Australian Institute of Criminology, 1988.

George, R. L. and Cristiani, T. S. (3rd ed.). *Counseling Theory and Practice.* Englewood Cliffs, N. J.: Prentice Hall, 1990.

Gesch, C. B., Hammond, S. M., Hampson, S. E., Eves, A. and Crowder, M. J. (2002). "Influence of Supplementary Vitamins, Minerals and Essential Fatty Acids on the Antisocial Behavior of Young Adult Prisoners." London: *British Journal of Psychiatry*, 181:22–8.

Gest, T. *Crime and Politics: Big Government's Erratic Campaign for Law and Order.* New York, NY: Oxford University Press, 2001.

Gibson, M. *Born to Crime: Cesare Lombroso and the Origins of Biological Criminology.* West Port, CT.: Praeger, 2002.

Gillespie, R. *Manufacturing Knowledge: A History of the Hawthorne Experiments.* Cambridge: Cambridge University Press, 1991.

Gilling, D. *Theory, Policy, and Politics*. London: Taylor & Francis Ltd, 1997.

Glaze, L. E. and Pella, S. "Probation and Parole in the United States, 2004." (2005) *Bureau of Justice Statistics Bulletin*. Washington DC: U. S. Department of Justice

Glenn Research Center. (2004) "Newton's Third Law of Motion." National Aeronautics and Space Administration: Cleveland, Ohio. Online: http://www.lerc.nasa.gov

Glueck, S. and Glueck, E. *Physique and Delinquency*. Boston: Houghton Mifflin, 1956.

Goffman, E. *Asylums: Essays on the Social Situation of Mental Patients and Other Inmates*. Garden City, N. Y.: Anchor, 1961.

Gongloff, M. (February 20, 2004) "Greenspan notes unease about jobs." Online: http:///www.CNN/Money

Gould, S. J. (1992) *The Confusion Over Evolution*. The New York Review of Books. November 19, 39–54.

Gould, S. J. (1997) *Darwinian Fundamentalism*. The New York Review of Books, June 12, 34–37.

Gould, S. J. *The Mismeasure of Man.* New York: W. W. Norton and Company, 1981.

Gregg V. Georgia 428 U. S. 153.

Gregor, M. (Ed). (2nd ed.). *The Metaphysics of Morals.* London: Cambridge University Press, 1996.

Grossman, L. S., Martis, B. and Fichtner, C. G. (March 1999) "Are Sex Offenders Treatable? A Research Overview." *Psychiatric Services,* 50 (3) 349–361.

Haigler, K. O., Harlow, C., O'Connor, P., and Campbell, A. (August 1993). *Adult Literacy in America: A First Look at the Findings of the National Adult Literacy Survey.* Washington DC: National Center for Education Statistics, U. S. Department of Education.

Hanson, R. K. and Bussiere, M. T. (1998) "Predicting Relapse: A Meta-Analysis of Sexual Offender Recidivism." *Journal of Clinical and Consulting Psychology,* 66 (2) 348–362.

Hare, R. D. *Without Conscience: the Disturbing World of Psychopaths.* New York, NY: Gulliford Publications, 1998.

Harer, M. D. (1995) "Recidivism Among Federal Prisoners Released in 1997." *Journal of Correctional Education*, 46(3), 98–128.

Hann, W. del. *The Politics of Redress: Crime, Punishment and Penal Abolition*. London: Unwin Hyman, 1990.

Harlow, C. W. *Education and Correctional Populations*. (January 2003). Washington DC: Bureau of Justice Statistics, U. S. Department of Justice.

Harp, G. J. *The Positivist Republic: Auguste Comte and the Reconstruction of American Liberalism, 1865–1920*. University Park, PA: Pennsylvania State University Press, 1995.

Harrington v. State of Iowa, 659 NW 2nd 509, 521 (2003).

Harris, R. A. *Creative Problem Solving: A Step-By-Step Approach*. Los Angles: Pyrczak Publishing, 2002.

Hedges, L. V. and Olkin, I. *Statistical Methods of Meta-Analysis*. New York, NY: Sage, 1985.

Herival, T. and Wright, P. (eds.) *Prison Nation: the Warehousing of America's Poor*. New York, NY: Routledge, 2003.

Herman, P. G. *The American Prison System*. New York, NY: H. W. Wilson Publishing Company, 2001.

Hirschi, T. *Causes of Delinquency*. Berkeley and Los Angles: University of California Press, 1969.

Hofer, P. J., Loeffler, C., Blakwell, K., and Valentino, P. (November 2004) *Fifteen Years of Guidelines Sentencing: An Assessment of How Well the Federal Criminal Justice System is Achieving the Goals of Sentencing Reform*. Washington DC: United States Sentencing Commission.

Hobbes, T. (W. Molesworth, ed.) Vol. 5. *The English Work of Thomas Hobbes*. London: Scientia Aalen, 1962.

Huff, C. R., Rattner, A. and Sagarin, E. (eds.) *Convicted But Innocent: Wrongful Conviction and Public Policy*, Thousand Oaks, CA: Sage Publication, 1996.

Hughes, K. A. (April 2006) *Justice Expenditures and Employment in the United States, 2003*. Washington DC: United States Department of Justice.

Hughes, K. A. (February 1992) *The Cost of Crime to Victims: Crime Data Brief*. Washington DC: United States Department of Justice.

Hunter, J. E., Schmidt, F. L., and Jackson, G. B. *Meta-Analysis: Cumulating Research Findings Across Studies*. Beverly Hills, CA: Sage, 1982.

Ip, G. "The gap in wages is growing again for U. S. workers." (January 23, 2004) *The Wall Street Journal*. Online: http//online.wsj.com/article

Ivey, A. E., D'Andrea, M., Ivey, M. B. and Simek-Morgan, L. (5th ed.). *Theories of Counseling and Psychotherapy*. Needham, MA: Allyn & Bacon, 2002.

Jeffery, C. R. *Crime Prevention Through Environmental Design*. Beverly Hills: Sage, 1971.

Johnson, B. R., Larson, D. B. and Pitts, T. C. (March 1997) "Religious Programs, Institutional Adjustment, and Recidivism Among Former Inmates in Prison Fellowship Programs." *Justice Quarterly*, 14 (1), 145–166

Johnston, N. B. *Forms of Constraint: A History of Prison Architecture*. Urbana, Ill.: University of Illinois Press, 2002.

Jones, M. D. *The Thinker's Toolkit: 14 Powerful Techniques for Problem Solving*. New York: Three Rivers Press, 1997.

Jones, W. H. (89th printing) *Nature of Man: Regimen in Health, Humors, Aphorisms. Cambridge, MA: Harvard University Press,* 1931.

Judd, D. K. *Taking Sides: Clashing Views on Controversial Issues in Religion.* Gilford, CT: McGraw Hill/Duskin, 2003.

Kagen, J. (Snidman, N., Arcus, D. Reznick, J. S. (collaborators). *Galen's Prophecy: Temperament in Human Nature.* New York: Basic Books, 1994.

Kalat. J. W. *Introduction to Psychology.* (4th ed.). Belmont, CA: Wadsworth, 2005.

Kaufman, P., Alt, M. N. and Chapman, C. D. (November 2004). *Dropout Rates in the United States: 2001.* Washington DC: National Center for Education Statistics.

Kennard, D. *An Introduction to Therapeutic Communities.* London: Jessica Kingsley Publishers, 1998.

Kennedy, Anthony M. Speech to the American Bar Association annual meeting. (August *9, 2003*). Online: http://www.suprecourtus.gov/publicinfo/ speeches/sp_08-09-03.

Kipp III, S. M., Price, D. V. and Wohlford, J. K. "Unequal Opportunity: Disparities in College Access Among the 50 States." *New Agenda Series*. Vol. 4. No. 3. Indianapolis: Lumina Foundation for Education, 2002.

Kirsch, I. S., Jungeblut, L. J., Kolstad, A. (August 1993) "A First Look at the Findings of the National Adult Literacy Survey. Washington DC: Department of Education.

Kitchner, P. *The Lives to Come: the Genetic Revolution and Human Possibilities*. New York: Simon & Schuster, 1997.

Kretschmer, Ernst. *Physique and Character: An Investigation of the Nature of Constitution and of the Theory of Temperament*. London: Routledge & Kegan, Paul Ltd., 1949.

Kutner, M., Greenberg, E. and Baer, J. (September 2003) *Adult Literacy: A First Look at Literacy of America's Adults in the 21st Century*. Washington DC: Department of Education

Langan, P. A., Schmitt, E. L. and Durose, M. R. *Recidivism of Sex Offenders Released from Prison in 1994*. (November 2003). Washington DC: Department of Justice.

Langan, P. A. and Levin, D. J. *Recidivism of Prisoners Released in 1994.* (June 2002) Washington DC: U. S. Department of Justice.

Langan, P. A. (1973) "Racism on Trial: New Evidence to Explain Racial Composition of Prisons in the United States." *Journal of Criminal Law and Criminology* 76 (3), 666–683.

Lawrence, S., Mears, D. P., Dubin, G., and Travis, J. (May 2002.) *The Practice and Promise of Prison Programming.* Washington DC: Urban Institute Justice Policy Center.

Laycock, G. (April 26, 2001). "Scientists or Politicians: Who Has the Answer to Crime?" Inaugural Address, Opening Ceremony, Jill Dando Institute of Crime Science, University College of London. London, England. Online: http://www.jdi.ucl.ac.uk/publications

Lazer, D. (ed.) *DNA Evidence and the Criminal Justice System: the Technology of Justice.* Cambridge, MA: MIT Press, 2004.

Lehmann, P. (Spring 2002) "Treatment-Induced Suicide: Suicidality as a Potential Effect of Psychiatric Drugs.

Journal of Critical Psychology, Counseling and Psychotherapy, 2 (1), 54–58.

Leichsenring, F. and Leibing, E. (July 2003) "The Effectiveness of Psychodynamic Therapy and Cognitive Behavior Therapy in the Treatment of Personality Disorders: A Meta-Analysis." *American Journal of Psychiatry*, 160: 1223–1232.

Lemert, E. *Social Pathology: A Systematic Approach to the Theory of Sociopathic Behavior*. New York, NY: McGraw-Hill, 1951.

Lewontin, R. C. (1979). "Sociobiology as an Adaptionist Program." *Behavioral Science*, 24, 5–14

Liberati, A. Journal of Epidemiology, Volume 48, Number 1, January 1995, pp. 81–86.

LoBuglio, S. (2000) "Time to Reframe Politics and Practices in Correctional Education." *The Annual Review of Adult Learning and Literacy*, Vol. 2, Chapter 4. Cambridge, MA: National Center for the Study of Adult Learning and Literacy.

Lyons, L. and Scheingold, S. (2000) "The Politics of Crime and Punishment. The Nature of Crime: Continuity and Change," *Criminal Justice*, 1, 103–149. Washington DC: National Institute of Justice.

MacCormick, A. H., *The Education of Adult Prisoners: Foundations of Criminal Justice*. New York, NY: AMS Press, 1931.

MacKenzie, D. L. "Results of a Multisite Study of Boot Camp Prison." (1994) Federal Probation, 58, (2), 60–66.

Maestro, M. T. *Voltaire and Baccaria as Reformers of Criminal Law*. New York: Octagon Books, 1972.

Mackay, C. *Schizophrenia and Other Psychotic Disorders*. Danvers, MA: Crown Publishing Group, 1995.

Maguire, K. and Pastore, A. L., (eds.) *Sourcebook of Criminal Justice Statistics, 2002* (2003)
Online: http://www.albany.edu/sourcebook.

Marshall, M. L. *Discipline Without Stress, Punishments or Rewards: How Teachers and Parents Promote Responsibility and Learning*. Los Alamitos, CA: Piper Press, 2002.

Martin, B. *Anxiety and Neurotic Disorders*. New York, NY: Wiley, 1971.

Mathieson, T. *Prison on Trial: A Critical Assessment*. Newbury Park, CA: Sage, 1990.

Mathieson, T. *The Politics of Abolition*. New York: Wiley, 1974.

McCarthy, J. C., Ross, C. F., Martoreelli, C. M. and Brown, (May 2004) A. "Near-Term Growth of Offshoring Accelerating: Realizing U.S. Services Jobs Going Offshore." Forrester Research.
Online: http://www.forresterresearch.com

Mead, G. H. *Mind, Self and Society*. Chicago: University of Chicago Press, 1934.

Meloy, J. R. *The Psychopathic Mind: Origins, Dynamics and Treatment*. Northvale: Jason Aronson Inc., 1988.

Mendez, M. F., Chen, A. K., Shapiro, J. S., Miller, B. L. (2005) "Acquired Sociopathy and Frontal Lobe Dementia." *Dementia and Geriatric Cognitive Disorders*, 20. (2–3), 99–104.

Menninger, K. *The Crime of Punishment.* New York: Viking, 1968.

Merton, R. "Social Structure and Anomie." *American Sociological Review* 3 (Oct. 1938): 672-682. Reprinted in *On Social Structure Science, essays by Robert K. Merton,* Piotr Sztompika, (ed.). Chicago: University of Chicago Press, 1996.

Meyers, G., *William James: His Life and Thoughts.* New Haven, CT: Yale University Press, 2001.

Miller, W. (1958) "Lower-Class Structure as a Generating Milieu of Gang Delinquency." *Journal of Social Issues,* 14, 9–30.

Mocan, H. N. and Gittings, R. K. *Pardons, Executions and Homicide.* (October 2001)
Online: http://www.econ.cudenver.edu/beckman/kai./pdf

Moore, David B. "Shame, Forgiveness, and Juvenile Justice." (Winter/Spring 1993) *Criminal Justice Ethics,* 12 (1) 3–25.

Morris, N. and Rothman, D. J. *The Oxford History of the Prison: the Practice of Punishment in Western Society*. New York, NY: Oxford University Press, 1998.

Morse, Stephen J. "Bad or Mad? Sex Offenders and Social Control." *Protecting Society from Sexually Dangerous Offenders: Law, Justice and Therapy*. Winick & LaFond (eds.) Washington DC: American Psychological Association, 2003.

Mumola, C. J. *Substance Abuse Treatment of State and Federal Prisoners*. (January 1999) Washington DC: Department of Justice.

Murphy, J. H. *Tracking and Location Technologies for the Criminal Justice System*. Pittsburgh: Westinghouse Electric Corporation, 1995.

Murphy, J. H. *Advanced Electronic Monitoring for Tracking Persons on Probation and Parole*. Pittsburgh: Westinghouse Science and Technology Center, 1994.

Nagel, W. G. *The Red Barn: A Critical Look at the Modern American Prison*. New York: Walker, 1973.

National Coalition for the Homeless. (May 2006) "How Many People Experience Homelessness?" NCH Fact Sheet #2. Online: http://www.nationalhomeless.org

Miller, T. R., Cohen, M. A. and Wiersema, B. (January 1996) *The Extent and Costs of Crime Victimization: A New Look*. Washington DC: U. S. Department of Justice.

National Low Income Housing Coalition. (February 2004) *America's Neighbors: the Affordable Housing Crisis and the People it Affects*.
Online: http://www.nlihc.org/research/neighbors

Neergaard, L. "FDA issues suicide caution for antidepressants." (March 22, 2004). Online: http://www.cnn.com

Newnes, C. (2002). "Speaking Out." *Ethical Human Sciences and Services* 3 (1), 135–142.

Newnes, C. (2000). "Can I see the test results please?" London: *The Guardian*.
Online: http://www.shropsych.org

Office of Management and Budget, (2006) *Presidential Budget Request for the Department of Justice*, Washington DC: Office of the President.

Oregon State Constitution, Article 1, Section 41.

Parent, D. G. (2003) *Correctional Boot Camps: Lessons from a Decade of Research*. Washington DC: National Institute of Justice.

Parker, K. F., DeWees, M. A. and Radelet, M. L. (Spring 2003) "Race, the Death Penalty, and Wrongful Convictions." *American Bar Association Criminal Justice* 18 (1), 48–54.

Pelissier, B., Wallace, S., O'Neil, J. A., Gaes, G. G., Camp, S., Rhodes, W., and Saylor (2001) "Federal Bureau of Prisons Residential Drug Treatment Reduces Substance Use and Arrest After Release." *Journal of Drug and Alcohol Abuse*, 27 (2), 315–337.

Pinker, S. *The Blank Slate: the Modern Denial of Human Nature*. New York: Penguin, 2002.

Pinker, S. *How the Mind Works*. New York: W W Norton & Company, 1999.

Pojman, L. P. (2004) "Why the Death Penalty is Morally Permissible." *Debating the Death Penalty: Should America*

Have Capital Punishment? H. Bedau and P. Cassel (eds.), New York, NY: Oxford University Press.

President's Commission on Law Enforcement and Administration of Justice, *Challenge of Crime in a Free Society* (1967) Washington DC: Department of Justice

Preston, D. L. and Murphy, S. (May 1997) "Motivating Treatment-Resistant Clients in Therapy." *Forum on Corrections Research*, 9 (2) 39–48.

Proctor, B. D. and Dalaker, J. (September 2003) *Poverty in the United States: 2002*. Washington DC: United States Bureau of the Census

Proussaint, A. F. and Alexander, A. *Lay My Burden Down: Unraveling Suicide and the Mental Health Crisis Among African-Americans*. Boston: Beacon Press, 2000.

Radelet, M. L., Hugo, Bedau, H. A. and Putnam, C. *In Spite of Innocence: Erroneous Convictions in Capital Cases*. Boston, MA: Northeastern University Press, 1992.

Raine, A. *The Psychopathology of Crime: Criminal Behavior as a Clinical Disorder*. San Diego, CA: Academic Press, 1993.

Raine, A., Loncz, T., Bihrle, S., LaCasse, L., Colletti, P. (2000) "Reduced Prefrontal Gray Matter Volume and Reduced Autonomic Activity in Antisocial Behavior." *Archives of General Psychiatry,* 57: 119–127.

Raphael, S. (2000). *The Deinstitutionalization of the Mentally Ill and Growth in the U. S. Prison Population: 1971 to 1996.* Berkeley: Goldman School of Public Policy, University of California.
Online: raphael@socrates.berkeley.edu

Reich, R. B. *The Work of Nations: Preparing Ourselves for 21st-Century Capitalism.* New York, NY: Alfred A. Knopf, Inc, 1991.

Reid, O. G., Mims, S. and Higginbottom, L. (2004). *Post-Traumatic Slavery Disorder: Definition, Diagnosis and Treatment.* Online: http://www.pyramidbuilders.org

Reynolds, T. (January 2004). "Youth signs papers agreeing to second-degree murder plea." St. Augustine: The St. Augustine Record

Rhee, S. H. and Waldman, I. (2002). "Genetic and Environmental Influences on Antisocial Behavior: A Meta-

Analysis of Twin and Adoption Studies." *Psychological Bulletin*, 128, (3), 490-529.

Rice, M. E. and Grant, T. H. "What We Know and Don't Know About Treating Sex Offenders." *Protecting Society from Sexually Dangerous Offenders: Law, Justice and Therapy.* (Winick & LaFond, eds.), Washington DC: American Psychological Association, 2003.

Riley, D. E. (1998). *DNA Testing: An Introduction for Non-Scientists—An Illustrated Explanation*.
Online: www.scientific.org/tutorials/articles/riley/riley.html

Robinson, M. B. *Why Crime? An Integrated Systems Theory of Antisocial Behavior.* Upper Saddle River, NJ: Prentice Hall, 2004.

Robinson, M. B. *Justice Blind? Ideals and Realities of American Criminal Justice.* Upper Saddle River, NJ: Prentice Hall, 2002.

Rosenbaum, D. P. (ed.) *Community Crime Prevention: Does It Work?* Beverly Hills: Sage, 1986.

Russell, M. J. (1993). *National Directory of Corrections: Construction Supplement.* Washington DC: National Institute of Justice.

Sabbatini, R. M. E. (1997). *Phrenology: the History of Brain Localization.* Brazil: State University of Campinas. Online: http://www.epub.org

Samenow, S. E. *Straight Talk About Criminals: Understanding and Treating Antisocials.* Northvale, NJ: Jason Aronson Publishers, 2002.

Schwitzgebel, R. K. (May 1969). "Issues in the Use of an Electronic Rehabilitation System with Chronic Recidivists." *Law & Society Review,* 7, 597–611.

Scott, J. "Rational Choice Theory." *Understanding Contemporary Society: Theories of the Present.* Browning, G., Halcli, A, Hewlett, N., and Webster, F. (eds.) London: Sage, 1999.

Sherman, L. W., Gottfredson, D., MacKenzie, D. Eck, J. Reuter, Bushway, S. in collaboration with members of the University of Maryland Graduate Program in Criminology and Criminal Justice. (1996). *Preventing Crime: What*

Works, What Doesn't, What's Promising. Washington DC: National Institute of Justice.

Shilton, M. K. "Balancing Correctional Costs to Improve Public Safety." The Center for Community Corrections, November 2000.

Skinner, B. F. *The Behavior of Organisms: An Experimental Analysis.* Acton, MA: Copley Publishing Group, 1999.

Slaughter v. Okalahoma OK CR2 105 P3d 832 (2205)

Sommer, R. *The End of Imprisonment.* New York: Oxford University Press, 1976.

Souter, C. R. (August/September 2003). "Theory: problems in black community traced to slavery."
Online: http://www.masspsy.com/leading/
0308_9_qa.html

Stephen, J. J. (June 2004) *State Prison Expenditures, 2001.* Washington DC: United States Department of Justice.

Stith, K. and Cabranes, J. A. *Fear of Judging.* Chicago: University of Chicago Press, 1998.

Sutherland, E. H. *White Collar Crime.* New York, NY: Holt, Rinehart and Winston, 1949.

Symons, D. (1992). "On the Use and Misuse of Darwinism in the Study of Human Behavior." *The Adapted Mind,* pp. 137–159.

Tannenbaum, F. *Crime and the Community.* NY: Columbia University Press, 1938.

Taylor, T. *The Haunting of America: Ghosts & Legends from America's Past.* Whitechapel Press: Alton, Illinois, 2001.

The National Commission for the Protection of Human Subjects of Biomedical and Behavioral Research. (April 1979) *Ethical Principles and Guidelines for the Protection of Human Subjects for Research.* Bethesda, Maryland: National Institute of Health

Thompson, K. (ed.) *Auguste Comte: the Foundation of Sociology.* New York: Wiley & Sons, 1976.

Thorndike, E. L. (2nd ed.) *Animal Intelligence: Experimental Studies.* New Brunswick, NJ: Transaction Publishers, 2000.

Thornhill, R. and Palmer, C. T. *A Natural History of Rape: Biological Bases of Sexual Coercion.* Cambridge, MA: MIT Press, 2000.

Tolbert, M. *State Correctional Education Programs.* (March 2002) Washington DC: National Institute for Literacy.

Tonry, M. and Petersila, J. (eds.). *Prisons: Crime and Justice,* Volume 26. Chicago: University of Chicago Press, 1999.

Tonry, M. and Farrington, D. P. (eds.) (1995). "Building a Safer Society: Strategic Approaches to Crime Prevention." *A Review of Research,* Vol. 19. Chicago: The University of Chicago Press

Toombs, T. G. "Monitoring and Controlling Criminal Offenders Using the Satellite Global Positioning System Coupled to Surgically Implanted Transponders: Is It a Viable Alternative to Prison?" (1996) *Criminal Justice Policy Review,* 7, (3-4/95) 341–346.

United States Bureau of the Census, (January 2005) *Population Estimates Program,* U. S. Department of Commerce: Washington DC.

United States Bureau of the Census, (August 2005) *Income, Poverty, and Health Insurance in the United States: 2005.* U. S. Department of Commerce: Washington DC.

United States Bureau of the Census, (July 2003). *Annual Estimates of the Population of the United States.* U. S. Department of Commerce: Washington DC.

United States Bureau of Justice Statistics, *Sourcebook of Criminal Justice Statistics, 2003*, (2005) Washington DC: U. S. Department of Justice.

United States Department of Agriculture (February 2004) *Amber Waves.* Online: http://www.ers.usda.gov

United States Department of Housing and Urban Development (October 2002) *American Housing Survey for the United States: 2001.* Online: http://www.usda.gov

United States Constitution.
Online: http://www.house.gov/Constitution/
Constitution.html

United States House of Representatives, Subcommittee on Technology, Environment, Aviation, Committee on Science, Space and Technology. (1994). "The Global

Positioning System: What Can't It Do? Hearing Report No. 102, One Hundred Third Congress, Second Session. Washington DC.

United States Office for the Protection from Research Risks, Institutes of Health, Department of Health and Human Services. (August 2001) *Title 45, Code of Federal Regulations, Part 46, Protection of Human Subjects.*

United States Sentencing Commission (USSC) (March 2006) *Final Report on the Impact of United States v Booker on Federal Sentencing.*

United States Supreme Court, *Roper v. Simmons*, U. S. 543, 2005.

United States Supreme Court, *Stanford v. Kentucky*, U. S. 361, 1989.

United States v. Booker, 543 U. S. 220, 2005

University of Washington School of Medicine. (June 2005) *Ethics in Medicine.*
Online: http://www.eduserv.hscer.washington.edu/ bioethics/topics/resrch.html

Van Wyhe, J. (2003). *The History of Phrenology on the Web.* Online: http://www.britishlibrary.net/phrenology/ overview

Wagner, S. F. *Introduction to Statistics.* New York, NY: Harper Collins, 1992.

Walsh, W. J. (Spring 1988). "Chemical Imbalances and Criminal Violence." *NOHA News*, XIII (2), 3-4.

Walsh, W. J. (Winter 1994). "Biochemistry and Behavior." *NOHA News*, XIX (1) 3–4.

Walters, J. P. (March 2001). *Drug Treatment in the Criminal Justice System.* Washington DC: Office of the President Office of National Drug Control Policy.

Westervelt, S and Humphrey, J. (eds.) *Wrongly Convicted: Perspectives on Failed Justice.* Piscataway, NJ: Rutgers University Press, 2001.

Wilbanks, W. *The Myth of a Racist Criminal Justice System.* Monterey, CA: Brooks Cole, 1987.

Williams, G. C. *Adaptation and Natural Selection: A Critique of Some Evolutionary Thought.* Princeton, NJ: Princeton University Press, 1966.

Wilson, D. B., Gallagher, C. A., and McKenzie, D. L. (2000) "A Meta-Analysis of Corrections-Based Education, Vocation, and Work Programs for Adult Offenders." *Journal of Research in Crime and Delinquency*, 37 (4), 347–368.

Wilson, E. O. *On Human Nature*. Cambridge, MA: Harvard University Press, 1978.

Wilson, E. O. "Introduction: What is Sociobiology?" *Sociobiology and Human Nature: An Interdisciplinary Critique and Defense*. Gregory, M. S., Silvers, A. and Sutch, D. (eds.) San Francisco, CA: Jossey-Bass, 1978.

Wilson, E. O. *Consilience: the Unity of Knowledge*. New York, NY: Vintage Books, 1999.

Wilson, J. Q. *Thinking About Crime*. New York: Random House, 1975.

Wilson, J. Q. and Herrnstein, R. *The Definitive Study of the Causes of Crime*. New York: Simon and Schuster, 1985.

Winick, B. J. and La Fond, J. Q. (eds.) *Protecting Society from Sexually Dangerous Offenders: Law, Justice and*

Therapy. Washington DC: American Psychological Association, 2003.

Wolfgard, M. and Ferracuti, F. *Subculture of Violence: Towards an Integrated Theory of Criminology.* New York, NY: Barnes & Noble, 1967.

Wright, R. A. *In Defense of Prisons.* Westport, Connecticut: Greenwood Press, 1994.

Yochelson, S. and Samenow, S. E. *Criminal Personality: A Profile for Change*, Vol. 1. Northvale, NJ: Jason Aronson Publishers, 1994.

Yochelson, S. and Samenow, S. E. *The Criminal Personality: the Change Process*, Vol. 2. Northvale, NJ: Jason Aronson Publishers, 1995.

Young, B. A. *Public High School Dropouts and Completers from the Common Core of Data: School Years 1998-99 and 1999-2000.* (August 2002) National Center for Education Statistics. U. S. Department of Education.

Zawidski, T. and Bechtel, W. (2004). "Gall's Legacy Revisited: Decomposition and Localization in Cognitive

Neuroscience."   Philosophy-Neuroscience-Psychology Program. St. Louis: Washington University.

978-0-595-41592-2
0-595-41592-X

www.ingramcontent.com/pod-product-compliance
Lightning Source LLC
Chambersburg PA
CBHW030253290526
45785CB00001B/69

* 9 7 8 0 5 9 5 4 1 5 9 2 2 *